DIANA
THE FASHION PRINCESS

DIANA
THE FASHION PRINCESS

Davina Hanmer

Photographs by
Tim Graham

An Owl Book

HOLT, RINEHART AND WINSTON
NEW YORK

Published in the United States by
Holt, Rinehart and Winston,
383 Madison Avenue, New York, New York 10017.

This book was designed and produced by
The Rainbird Publishing Group Ltd
40 Park Street, London W1Y 4DE.

Library of Congress Cataloging in Publication Data

Hanmer, Davina.
   Diana, the fashion princess.
   "An owl book."
   1. Diana, Princess of Wales, 1961–   —Clothing.
2. Great Britain—Princes and princesses—Biography.
3. Fashion—History—20th century. I. Title.
DA591.A45D5317 1984   941.085′092′4 [B]   84-570
ISBN: 0-03-072068-0

First American Edition

Text set by Type Gallery Ltd, London, England
Colour origination by Bridge Graphics Ltd, Hull, England
Printed and bound by Severn Valley Press, Caerphilly, Wales

10 9 8 7 6 5 4 3 2 1

FRONTISPIECE: The Princess of Wales at Shelburne during the
Tour of Canada in June 1983. With her black felt sombrero she
is wearing a bright red Jasper Conran suit and black and white
spotted shirt with a soft pussy cat bow at the neck.

ILLUSTRATION ACKNOWLEDGMENTS

All the photographs in this book were taken by Tim
Graham except the following: *Theo Bergstrøm* page 36
(above); *Camera Press Ltd* pages 11/Glenn Harvey, 13
(left)/Glenn Harvey, 21/LNS, 25 (left)/Snowdon, 34/
Lichfield, 36 (below), 49 (right)/Glenn Harvey, 92/Glenn
Harvey, 95 (left)/Jim Bennett, 106 (above)/Bryn Colton,
114 (left)/Snowdon, 117/Joe Bulaitis, 122 (above)/Glenn
Harvey, 122 (below)/Snowdon, 124 (above and below)/
Snowdon, 126 (above) John Scott, 126 (below)/Snowdon,
128/Portrait painting by June Mendoza; *Colour Library
International* pages 19 (right), 23 (right), 35 (above), 102;
London Express News and Features Services page 19 (left);
Lynn News and Advertiser page 15 (below); *The Press
Association Ltd* (Photos The Rainbird Publishing Group)
pages 14, 15 (above), 37, 39; *Sir Geoffrey Shakerley* page
17 (above); *Syndication International* pages 25 (right), 38.

ISBN 0-03-072068-0

CONTENTS

Author's preface

To write a proper book, as opposed to a lengthy article, on the fashion of the Princess of Wales seemed a daunting task. How could I write at length about the clothes of however beautiful a girl who has only been in the public eye for a little over two years? I consulted my many colleagues in the fashion business and other fashion writers and came up with as many different ideas. In the end, I disregarded their multifarious advice and struck out on talking to as many people as possible connected with the Princess's extensive wardrobe and formed my own opinions from there on. Consequently, I have tried throughout the text to imagine that I was meeting the Princess for the first time at each of her official engagements and write objectively from that angle alone. From then on, my task was easy and a joy to record how an inexperienced but fashion-conscious young woman developed into one of the best dressed women in the world, albeit not without making the odd mistake.

Becoming a princess does not guarantee that an ordinary girl is transformed into a glamorous fairy-tale beauty but this *is* what happened to the Princess of Wales. In real life, the transformation occurs, not with the wave of a magic wand, not even because of a greatly increased dress allowance, but through the hard work and judgment of many creative and experienced designers.

When the Princess comes into a room for a formal dinner or some other function there is almost always a gasp of surprise and pleasure. Fashion writers hurry to record her new tastes in clothes and before long the clothes she likes are imitated and reinterpreted in a thousand stores across the country.

Here, after considerable research, I have traced this fascinating story, the story that lies behind 'the magic wand'. There will always be fashion writers who will not like what they see the Princess wear, but for me and for millions of others, the Princess of Wales, through a sensible but also daring and imaginative approach to fashion, has brought glamour and excitement into a world too often dreary and dull.

Finally, I would like to thank those fashion houses who put up with my incessant queries, in the interest of accuracy, and for their inestimable help.

The Princess of Wales during the tour of Australia, wearing a striking blue and white, floral-printed dress made by Donald Campbell.

There can be few who could have prophesied in the euphoria of the Royal Wedding that the Princess of Wales would make quite such a name for herself, throughout the world and quite so soon. Yet this young woman, still in her very early twenties, is hailed as an ambassadress for youth, beauty and style. Whenever she is seen in public, be it on a Royal Tour to a Commonwealth country, a State occasion or just a day visit to a factory in the Midlands or to her local children's adventure playground, she never fails to delight all those whom she meets or those who have flocked to see her. To them, and to millions around the world, she is everything that they demand of a modern-day princess. Wherever she goes, her reputation precedes her and no one is disappointed. They love her for her charm, her beauty, her warm smile, her simple 'common touch' – all real attributes that are truly complemented by the way she dresses, clothes chosen with thought and care for each special occasion. At the times when she is seen 'off duty', her fresh approach to her less formal wardrobe is just as appealing.

Today, the fashion magazines the world over compete for new articles on her and her clothes, for they well know what a front-cover photograph of the Princess of Wales can do to their sales. The fashion houses also revel in the Princess for they recognize her invaluable contribution to the revival of the British fashion industry. Annette Worsley Taylor – the founder of the London Designer Collection – says of her, 'She is one of the most fashion-conscious women in the world. When she popularised her "romantic look", which fitted in so well with her engagement and wedding, she was really following London fashion. Now our fashion has become sleeker and more sophisticated, the Princess has changed with it. She always dresses British and everywhere she goes people know this. It couldn't be better for us.' There are, however, many non-British designers who design for the Princess of Wales, such as Donald Campbell from Canada, Jan Van Velden from Holland or Catherine Walker, founder of The Chelsea Design Company, who is French. They all have British fashion houses within the United Kingdom and as such, can be classed as 'British'.

The Princess of Wales never fails to monitor her own success, and she takes a great interest in seeing how her clothes photograph. She is never slow to take advice on the styles and colours that do not suit her and she is well aware of what 'being tall' means, what she can and cannot wear. With this valuable experience, she is slowly building an individual style of her own. Although she is moving on and experimenting with new styles and colours in her clothes, following the current fashion trends, she has

FACING PAGE: *Wearing a slim-fitting, classic double-breasted coat in grey worsted with a faint chalk stripe, the Princess of Wales leaves Aberdeen airport with Prince William on their way back from Balmoral. The choice of cloth, the contrasting velvet collar and style of coat are typical of the Princess's stylish taste.*

remained faithful to her original hairstyle of long, layered hair, almost her trade mark, as opposed to the now more fashionable straighter, flatter look.

The beneficial effect of the Princess of Wales's interest in fashion has been felt financially by the hard-pressed fashion industry. Prince Charles, too, has come into her 'fashion aegis'. For years, to the chagrin of his tailor, he has been sartorially staid and has invariably worn his suits badly. With the Princess's direct intervention, he has become far more adventurous with his clothes. (His valet of

This smart, striped tailored suit in seersucker was designed by Bruce Oldfield, one of the Princess of Wales's most imaginative designers. It was worn by the Princess to visit the Queen Mother at Clarence House on the occasion of her 83rd birthday. For this private visit she is wearing higher heels than she normally chooses.

FACING PAGE: *For this visit to Bedford, the Princess of Wales wears an especially striking emerald-green, three-quarter length suit designed by Jasper Conran in his classic style. With it, she wears a white silk blouse with mandarin collar and a favourite three-stranded pearl choker with turquoise clasp.*

BELOW: *Always ready to surprise and delight her many admirers, the Princess of Wales rose to the occasion of a pop concert at the Royal Albert Hall in September 1983 by wearing a dazzling silver suit designed by Bruce Oldfield. Her simple court shoes and clutch evening handbag were also in silver.*

many years left soon after the Royal Wedding.) He is now wearing more double-breasted suits, including dinner jackets, and his other suits are cut in a more dashing line. He wears his hair longer and it is now cut by her hairdresser, Kevin Shanley. Although the press are quick to extend the sartorial influence of the Princess of Wales to baby clothes as well, Prince William is dressed in an identical fashion to every other baby whose parents can afford the range of clothes available in the more expensive shops.

Whatever the fashion pundits say of the Princess of Wales and her clothes, she has shown that she has a certain style and flair of her own and she is not afraid to show it. She has shown that she can dress for a special occasion, be it a sad funeral, or an exciting pop festival, such as the dazzling silver suit with matching handbag and shoes that she wore for a pop concert at the Royal Albert Hall in aid of the Prince's Trust in September 1983. She is fully aware that she is the centre of attention wherever she is seen in public and she is not reticent in rising to the occasion, such as her two off-the-shoulder evening dresses worn at a time when her critics were calling her 'dowdy'. It is no wonder that she continues to be voted top of the British Best Dressed Women polls year after year, also in Ireland and El Salvador too.

The meteoric rise of Lady Diana Spencer, a teenage kindergarten helper – albeit an aristocratic one – dressed exactly like her contemporaries, to the sparkling heights of the Princess of Wales's current position as one of the top ten best-dressed women in the world, is a testimony to her deep love of clothes, her interest in fashion and her remarkable ability to make whatever she is wearing look absolutely *right*. This success is due not so much to any inherent dress sense – to the professionals she is still a gifted novice in the way she puts her clothes together – but to her ability to wear those clothes to their best advantage.

Queen Victoria maintained that 'Dress is a trifling matter, but it gives also the outward sign from which people in general can, and often do, judge upon the inward state of mind and feeling of a person.' So it is with the Princess of Wales. Initially, it is her shining personality that gives the overall, pleasing effect; the clothes she is wearing, however stunning, are secondary. She is no clothes-horse, no mere couturier's model.

The Princess of Wales is young and fresh. She is tall, 5 feet 10¼ inches, with a near perfect figure and good bone structure. Hers is a supreme, classic beauty – the fairest hair, the deepest blue eyes and the softest of 'English' complexions. She is conscious of her slim figure and weight, some say overconscious, but who cannot marvel at the difference between the Lady Diana Spencer of her engagement photographs and the Princess of Wales of today, elegant far beyond her tender years. She aims to keep her figure too; she is faithful to a strict diet – at official functions she only nibbles at her food and never drinks alcohol, even at home. She has always kept herself exceptionally fit, attending ballet classes in the early days, but, since the birth of Prince

At the photocall just before Christmas 1983 in the private gardens of Kensington Palace, the proud mother leads Prince William forward to face the cameras. The Princess of Wales's clothes are typical of those worn by her on off-duty days – comfortable but stylish.

the longer skirts fit in admirably with her style on her 'walkabouts', where she is continually bending down to talk to children or leaning forward to talk and shake hands with those in the back of a crowd. A shorter skirt would simply ride up her legs, and she well knows the penchant of the *paparazzi* to catch the flash of a petticoat or the outline of her legs backlit by the sun. The choice of the colour she wears or the style of hat is not entirely hers either. Whatever the colour in fashion at the time, she must dress to be seen. Her hats must show her pretty face; colours must be distinguishable to the crowd, even on a grey day, and, above all, photograph well.

The Princess of Wales is invariably dubbed as a leader of fashion – despite her only title, The Princess of Wales, the tag 'the Lady Di look' has remained. A leader of fashion is an innovator, someone with a style of their own and that style is then copied. The Princess of Wales is young but she is learning. She has good advisers, the top fashion editors from *Vogue*, but she is still feeling her way through volumes of fabrics and experimenting with different lines and colours. She has yet to develop a distinct style of her own.

In the words of The Kinks, the sixties pop group, she is 'a dedicated follower of fashion'. The original 'Lady Di look', the 'ruffled shirts with ribbons at the neck, baggy jumpers with straight skirts or jeans, a touch of ethnic', knickerbockers and flat shoes, was simply what every girl of her age and background was wearing at that time. She was a typical young 'Sloane Ranger', a girl with a life style and invariable wardrobe as exemplified in a *Harpers and Queen* magazine article, later expanded into a book. After Lady Diana was seen in the Prince of Wales's company at Balmoral, photographs of her, and hence her clothes, were seen in every newspaper in the world as they have been ever since. From that moment on, the 'young Sloane Ranger' style started its 'gallop down the high streets' and the 'Lady Di look' was in. It was a style that was easily, and inexpensively, copied and its success to the manufacturers was somewhat reminiscent of the early Carnaby Street days. The original 'Sloanes', unamused by the pastiche, merely replied that that fashion was on the way 'out' for them anyway.

Today, the majority of the Princess of Wales's clothes are more difficult to copy as her couturier-designed clothes rely more heavily on the quality of the material and the cut and are thus relatively uncommercial for the mass market. However, many of her clothes are still copied. Her white Victorian-style blouses with the pie-frilled collars became an instant success. Lyn Morris, Senior Selector for Marks and Spencer Ladies' Blouses, recalled that 'as soon as Diana did that engagement picture, our fastest-selling style was a side-tying Lady Di blouse'. It sold for £9.99. Some of her summer clothes, like her range of cotton maternity dresses with white collars, are now appearing in the high-street shops. At the other end of the market, the more expensive copies have a ready market, particularly abroad.

William, she has followed Jane Fonda's exercises in her workout book. She also makes full use of the swimming pools at Highgrove, Buckingham Palace and Windsor Castle. Although her figure is the envy of most women, her posture is not good. In common with most tall women, she is inclined to stoop, and this, coupled with her broad shoulders, tends to lower the bust line and so hinder the natural flow of the material of her dress.

It is indeed fortunate that the Princess of Wales is intensely interested in fashion, for much time and forethought go into the way she dresses for each of her official duties. It is not an easy task. She has to combine what is pleasing to her, what is practical and, obviously, what is acceptable for someone in her position – the vagaries of the weather are not least in the choice of material. Tact in her clothes is also appreciated – the tartans and the tam o' shanters she wears in Scotland or, for the tour of Wales, a coat made out of wool from the Principality. Some critics maintain that the 'Palace' influence is too heavy on one so young, that her clothes are too classical, too dowdy and the hems too long. Incidentally, as far as those hem lengths are concerned, the Princess of Wales is 'in fashion' and

Although the Princess of Wales cannot be classed as a leader of fashion in the accepted sense, she has undeniably influenced the fashion-conscious public by simply wearing such a wide variety of clothes, colours and accessories. Because of how she dresses, she has inspired others to expand their ideas and their wardrobes. For example, it is nonsense to suggest that more women are wearing hats because the Princess of Wales has made them fashionable – a hat is the correct *tenue* for her daytime engagements; she, of course, wears one that usually complements whatever she is wearing. However, because of the rich variety of style and colour of the Princess's hats, fashion-conscious women today are inspired by her lead and take just that more time and trouble when they themselves come to choose a hat.

The top couturiers who are brought to her attention count themselves fortunate to have such royal patronage. They admire her for the fact that she is prepared to try out the many fashion houses – unlike the Queen, who, confident in her designers, goes almost exclusively to three salons, Hardy Amies, Norman Hartnell and Ian Thomas. They also admire the Princess of Wales for her courage in departing from the norm from the outset, such as the choice of David and Elizabeth Emanuel for her wedding dress, which surprised many of the more established fashion houses. The Princess's new salons, however, do enjoy an instant popularity, a boost not always totally welcome as it overloads their workrooms and is damaging to their reputations if the Princess were to move on elsewhere. Exactly what the Princess's clothes actually cost is a secret between her, the Prince of Wales who pays from his sizeable income from the Duchy of Cornwall, the fashion house and Coutts, the Royal Bankers. However, they are somewhere between 'full price' and 'cost'. Collectively, these designers, with their centuries of fashion experience behind them, agree that their young client is still developing her individual style. Individually, each one hopes that in the not too distant future, theirs will be the salon to display,

'By Appointment to HRH The Princess of Wales.'

However, where those same pundits are calling for her to *set* a fashion, the Princess of Wales knows full well that she has no need, for those whom she meets and who come to see her, are delighted with whatever she is wearing and that is all that matters to her.

For Christmas Day 1983, the Princess of Wales chose to wear a most elegant cream suit with a striking jabot down the front and a hat in the same cream. The whole effect was enlivened by splashes of maroon – in the handkerchief of the jacket breast pocket, the eye veil and the sweep of her hat.

For the second year running, the Prince and Princess of Wales managed to take a short skiing holiday, staying in Liechtenstein with the reigning family. Ever fashionable even when on the ski slopes, the Princess wears a smart plum-coloured all-in-one ski suit to keep warm on the bitterly cold snowy morning.

EARLY LIFE

There is always a note of expectation, a hint of expectation, a hint of excitement with a murmur of surprise for those who go to see or follow the fashion of the Princess of Wales. Not so her early clothes and her teenage choice of fashion, which were entirely predictable, being indistinguishable from the thousands of other girls of her age, class and background.

Where fashion and clothes are all important to some precocious little girls, to the Honourable Diana Spencer they were of little interest. With two sisters, Sarah six years and Jane just four years older, Diana, had she thought about it, could have seen exactly what she would be wearing when she reached their size. These 'hand me downs' were almost the uniform of the children of 'the county set' – even more so with the Spencer children as Norfolk, where Diana lived in a house in the grounds of the royal residence of Sandringham, is still considered somewhat feudal and sartorially traditional.

Diana's day clothes were entirely practical. Weather permitting, days were spent out of doors, in the garden, on her parents' two farms or on the beach with family and pets. Like every other small girl, she wore little dresses or shorts, a shirt and a sweater, and when slightly older, the ubiquitous jeans – cotton trousers in the summer – when she grew up into something of a 'tomboy'.

Sunday or best clothes were always smart, well made, often expensive, and invariably of the highest quality – they had to be if they were to last through three daughters. Diana's mother, the then Lady Althorp, bought the clothes for all the children, using London shops such as Harrods, Debenham and Freebody in Wigmore Street and The White House and Rowes (now merged). Her smarter clothes included little dresses with smocking on the front and the essential Harris Tweed coat with a stitched velvet collar, covered buttons and a half belt at the back. For weddings, such as her uncle Lord Fermoy's in 1964, or other society weddings in Norfolk, a large but simple straw hat was added that well suited the pretty and engaging little girl. For parties, Diana had a selection of dresses, some inherited from her sisters, others bought especially for her. These she wore with white socks and ballet shoes to the many children's parties of her neighbours and cousins or dancing classes held in the Christmas holidays.

This fully functional, smart, but not overlarge, wardrobe of Diana's was supervised by her mother but looked after by her nanny, Judith Parnell, a young girl from Kent. She, and subsequent nannies, were responsible for all her clothes. The washing and

FACING PAGE: *As a young girl the Princess of Wales was always neat and tidy, wearing simple but practical clothes for the outdoor life she preferred. She is seen here at the age of thirteen on the Isle of South Uist in the Outer Hebrides of Scotland during one school holiday from West Heath. Her comfortable clothes were typical of those worn by girls of her age when in the country, a check shirt worn with a Shetland sweater and a green quilted Husky waistcoat topped by a tweed hat.*

TOP: *The Honourable Diana Spencer photographed on the lawns of Park House, Sandringham on her first birthday. Dressed for the occasion she wears a pretty, broderie anglaise dress laced with pink ribbon.*

ABOVE: *Diana at her uncle Lord Fermoy's wedding in 1964 when she was nearly three years old. Dressed in her best clothes she is wearing a large straw hat, her Sunday coat, white cotton socks and polished button shoes.*

ironing was done by a daily helper, but nanny did the mending, sewed on name tapes and, later, packed the trunk for school.

The day came, in January 1968, when the seven-and-a-half-year-old Diana was sent to Silfield, a day school in nearby King's Lynn. Each morning she would dress in her school uniform of a grey skirt, red jumper and tights in the winter and a red check gingham dress and red cardigan in the summer. It was a practical uniform which Diana liked, but as soon as school was over and homework done, it was time to change back into old clothes. As neither Sarah nor Jane had been to Silfield, or to her next school, Riddlesworth Hall in Norfolk, Diana had a brand-new uniform. She was taken to Harrods, the school's outfitters, by her mother, and so began a long association between her and the store.

In keeping with most girls' schools, Riddlesworth has a comprehensive list that includes grey pleated skirts, white Aertex shirts for weekdays, blue and white checked gingham shirts for Sundays, cherry twin sets, a dozen linen handkerchiefs and nine pairs of knickers (six inner and three outer). Diana did not mind conforming to the school uniform although, like the hundreds of girls that have been through that school, her Sunday clothes were somewhat of a trial – the cherry-red dress known as 'prickles', thick stockings known as 'elephant hides', the severe, felt hat and grey coat, gloves and heavy walking shoes.

At the age of twelve, Diana followed her two sisters to West Heath, a select boarding school in Kent. It was an admirable school, where the headmistress, Miss Ruth Rudge, believed in 'fostering the individuality of each of her pupils' and encouraged them to develop their 'own minds and tastes'. For those very reasons, the girls were allowed to wear what they liked after lessons on weekdays and at the weekends (the school uniform was a simple navy skirt, white blouse, navy cardigan and a tie, blue with a silver stripe). An old girl remembered that, 'West Heath was a departure from most other girls' schools in the area as we were instantly distinguishable in church by the fact that we were the only ones in our own clothes. They were all very jealous of us.' Miss Rudge particularly remembers Lady Diana, as she became on the accession of her father as eighth Earl Spencer in 1975, wearing a pair of bright red dungarees. Later, she confided, 'The way she dresses now is just an extension of the way she dressed here. She had a sense of colour and was meticulous about the way she looked. It was natural to her – she's a neat, tidy person, and simple. She always dressed simply, but there was a bit of distinction about her even if she was wearing jeans and doing a bit of the weeding.' Weeding was a favourite punishment of the headmistress.

During her time at West Heath, she became more interested in fashion. She chose her own clothes in the holidays and to her, the fashion page of *The Daily Telegraph* and the glossy magazines at home became essential reading. A tall girl for her age, Lady Diana was soon borrowing her sisters' clothes rather than 'inheriting' them. As both Sarah and Jane were working in London, later for *Vogue*, the three sisters were very much in touch with the fashion world.

After Lady Diana left West Heath at the age of sixteen, she went to a finishing school at Château d'Oex in Switzerland, with some borrowed clothes for skiing, before returning to England in time for her sister Jane's wedding, where she was chief bridesmaid. The bridesmaids' dresses, printed cream and red, long pinafore dresses trimmed in red, were designed and hand made by Bill Pashley. Jane had met him at a wedding, liked his work and later commissioned him to make her bridesmaids' dresses. To Pashley, known as 'Battersea Bill' or 'Mr Frantic Frocks', society weddings are the ultimate. He admits that he 'loves brides' and bridesmaids' dresses. It's a challenge because you've got a captive audience staring at the bride's back.' This dress was the first of many that Pashley was to make for Lady Diana. She was to be a bridesmaid just once more, in May 1980, to her elder sister, Sarah, where she wore a three-quarter length silk skirt and frilled blouse.

Schooling over, Lady Diana moved to London. At first, she borrowed her mother's flat, but then was given a flat of her own, in Coleherne Court, in South Kensington, which she shared with three friends. Her London life, and wardrobe, was simply an extension of her country life and, along with her flatmates and all their friends, she dressed in a thoroughly predictable style as befitted her allowance, background and taste. Lady Diana was the archetypal 'young Sloane Ranger' – according to *The Official Sloane Ranger Handbook*, the book that grew from an article in *Harpers and Queen* magazine, she knew 'what mattered most' and, accordingly, 'how to dress'. In fact, she wore what she liked, what was most comfortable and what suited her, and it was that choice that neatly coincided with the fashion of her set.

The insignia of the Sloane Ranger is the silk scarf, knotted round the neck of the younger Sloanes (as opposed to knotted under the chin of the older), the single string of pearls, the navy blue velvet jacket, the pleated or straight skirts, culottes (invariably navy), knickerbockers, handbag, low-heeled shoes (both expensive) and pale tights. Such 'livery' could be bought from shops such as Simpson's of Piccadilly, Harvey Nichols or Jaeger and Gucci, Bally or Rayne for the bags and shoes. Dressed in such a way, with only minor variations such as her borrowed man's corduroy jacket, Lady Diana was perfectly dressed for any smart daytime venue.

In early September 1980, a journalist and a photographer from a tabloid newspaper were watching the Prince of Wales fish on the River Dee, which runs through the Balmoral Estate, the Queen's home in the Highlands of Scotland. They were surprised by the flash of the sun on a hand mirror held out from behind a tree and the tip of a green Wellington boot. As they moved in, a girl sprinted up a hill and away. All they had was a description of her clothes – a man's cap pulled down over a knotted headscarf,

TOP: *Diana was chief bridesmaid (standing back right) at her sister Lady Jane's wedding in 1978. This was the first time that Diana came across the designer, Bill Pashley, who made the dresses for the bride and bridesmaids. The printed cream and red, long pinafores complemented the red and gold salon at St James's Palace.*

ABOVE: *Bill Pashley with his beagle, Sybil, at his home in Battersea, south London. Alone among the top designers, Bill Pashley not only designs but prefers to cut and sew all his garments himself. The bridesmaid's dress was the first of many clothes to be made for Diana during the next few years and especially during her engagement.*

LEFT AND RIGHT: *With her inherent sense of colour and style the Princess of Wales has always made everyday clothes look that much more chic. During the months before her engagement when she was harassed daily by journalists and photographers she always managed to look poised and stylish, wearing (left) a simple turquoise*

cotton shirt enhanced by a jaunty scarf, a pair of turquoise, enamel earrings and the famous mark of a Sloane Ranger, a single string of well-matched pearls, and (right) a velvet jacket in a favourite colour of deep red with a black rollneck jumper and the simplest of gold hoop earings.

check shirt, chunky sweater, slim corduroys and the green Hunter Wellingtons. Later, they were able to identify the girl, who was, of course, Lady Diana. Her clothes on that occasion, her normal wear for the country, again coincided with the 'Sloane' look — other 'essential' items of hers were a Husky (a green quilted waistcoat or jacket), a Barbour (a thick, thornproof raincoat, also in green), a lodenmantel, for London and the country, flowered cotton skirts from Laura Ashley, various brightly coloured ethnic sweaters, some from Inca, a shop in London's Pimlico, other lamb's-wool sweaters from Benetton and cardigans from Friends.

After that initial sighting in Scotland, Lady Diana was pursued remorselessly by the press and their photographers. Her limited wardrobe was seen in every combination, mostly intercepted as she went to work or home from some party. They 'caught' her wearing her lodenmantel over the coral-pink evening dress that she wore for Princess Margaret's birthday party at the Savoy (one of the first

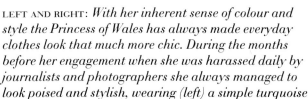

FACING PAGE: *The working clothes of the typical Sloane Ranger – Lady Diana Spencer photographed in the gardens beside the kindergarten school in Pimlico where she worked until the announcement of her engagement. Her informal but practical clothes consisted of many light cotton skirts with matching, coloured shirts and tops.*

occasions that she appeared with Prince Charles in public) which had been bought from Tatters in the Fulham Road, not far from her flat. As very much a working girl, she dressed practically for her various jobs. She has worn jeans all her life, bought at that time from shops such as Fiorucci, Benetton and Jean Machine. On her long legs, they looked just that much more chic than the run-of-the-mill blue jeans. Jeans, which were perfectly acceptable for her job as a kindergarten helper in the mornings and part-time nanny in the afternoons, were worn with the ruffled shirts with ribbons at the neck that were to become her hallmark (bought from shops such as Laura Ashley), cardigans and baggy, colourful sweaters that she had found in shops such as Brother Sun in London's Fulham Road. Brother Sun also supplied her rope-soled espadrilles in many bright colours and her quilted bags in Provençal cotton.

As the romance blossomed, Lady Diana had to increase her wardrobe, sometimes by borrowing, to keep up with her position as the girlfriend of the Prince of Wales. One of her chief pleasures then, and now, is shopping for clothes, although she obviously does not have that same anonymity, hence freedom, today. Hers was a well-worn route, known in 'Sloane Ranger' parlance as the 'tiara triangle', bounded by Harrods, across to Harvey Nichols and down to Sloane Square.

ENGAGEMENT

In February of the next year, 1981, the engagement was officially announced and Lady Diana was well, although not over, prepared. An early fashion mentor of hers was her mother, now the Honourable Mrs Peter Shand Kydd. As no one expected to see the future Princess of Wales actually out walking in the streets, she and her mother did most of her clothes shopping on foot. Striding out with their long legs and heads bowed, no one recognised them.

Her engagement day started at half past eight with an appointment with her hairdresser of nearly four years' standing, Kevin Shanley, at his salon Head Lines in South Kensington. Sensing a special day, he gave her hair his best attention, following her original style that was to be tagged 'the Lady Di look' from that day on. To meet the Court correspondents in the morning she had chosen a deep red velvet suit, the ubiquitous ruffled blouse, red tights and low-heeled shoes. For the Princess of Wales, the height of her shoes is always vital, as, according to official sources, the Prince of Wales is a quarter of an inch taller than his wife but in fact he is marginally the shorter. The world was not to see the difference in height at their first official appearance in public as they posed on the garden steps of Buckingham Palace together, Prince Charles standing one step higher. It was a charming photograph, she in the now famous sapphire blue silk suit with scalloped edges and matching belt with a bow. The suit was designed by Cojana, a British fashion house with an international reputation (they had won a Queen's Award for Exports the previous year), and bought 'off the peg' not long before the announcement. With it, she wore a white silk blouse with a blue swallow motif. That evening, the crowds who had been waiting outside Clarence House, the Queen Mother's residence where Lady Diana was by then staying, were rewarded with a glimpse of her in a long Chinese silk skirt embroidered with chrysanthemums, white lace-trimmed blouse, a three-strand pearl choker and the happiest of smiles.

As the fiancée of the Prince of Wales, Lady Diana's clothes became even more crucial and more minutely examined. Once again, this girl of nineteen rose to the occasion and carried off her new position with a wardrobe to match with aplomb and confidence. Although the final choice was hers, she did have some expert advice to guide her through the maze of the *haute couture* houses. Her mother was there to introduce her daughter to her favourite salons, but help also came from the top of the fashion world. Before their marriages, Lady Sarah and Lady Jane Spencer both worked for *Vogue* and had retained their ties with the staff of the magazine. The Editor-in-Chief, Beatrix Miller, the Fashion Editor, Grace Coddington (the famous former model), and

her deputy, Anna Harvey, with Felicity Clark, the Beauty Editor, were all brought in for their expert advice. Between them, they had the right experience and could be trusted to be discreet. Above all, they knew the designers, their work and what was available in which shops. As literally thousands of new creations from all the top designers were sent to *Vogue*'s offices in Hanover Square for possible inclusion in the magazine, it gave Lady Diana the ideal chance to 'window shop' and to try on clothes without the hindrance of a fascinated, but nonetheless staring, crowd whenever she went out shopping. Today, the same arrangement with the magazine exists, although Anna Harvey is the sole *Vogue* 'adviser'. Also, general shopping is now more difficult for the Princess of Wales, although she does manage to slip into the larger stores such as Harrods and Harvey Nichols in the early morning without causing too much of a commotion.

In the months before her wedding, Lady Diana had the daunting task of choosing clothes for herself. Not only did she have to choose her wedding dress and trousseau but also all the clothes for the private and official functions during the engagement, the holiday in Scotland and their Royal Tour of Wales.

For her first official engagement with Prince Charles Lady Diana wore a sensational black silk taffeta evening dress with matching wrap made by the Emanuels. Although similar in style and colour to one worn by the Queen at the time of her own engagement, the press described it as a daring choice.

LEFT: *For the famous photocall on the afternoon of her engagement Lady Diana wore a sapphire blue silk suit with scalloped edges and a white silk blouse with a blue, swallow motif. The suit was made by a London fashion house, Cojana, and had been bought from Harrods.*

The black silk taffeta evening dress that Lady Diana wore for her first official engagement with her fiancé, a music and verse recital at the Goldsmith's Hall in the City of London, revealed much of, and about, the future Princess of Wales. Although the dress was similar to one that the Queen, as Princess Elizabeth, had worn at the time of her engagement in 1947, it was a daring choice, as the strapless top and plunging neckline revealed bare shoulders and a deep cleavage. When she arrived at the Hall, 'no one dared breathe for fear the lady would lose her all'. The photograph of her in the Iranian edition of *Time* magazine had her bare shoulders blacked in. The choice of that dress also demonstrated from the outset that, as far as her clothes were concerned, she had a mind of her own and she was determined to use it.

'That dress', as it became known, had been made some time previously by David and Elizabeth Emanuel, a young husband and wife design team with a salon just off Bond Street in the heart of London's *haute couture* land. Earlier, Lady Diana had been asked to be photographed by Lord Snowdon for a *Vogue* feature in a pink chiffon blouse with a high, frilled neck. The blouse was exactly her style and she telephoned her friends on the magazine to find out the name of the designer. On finding that it was the Emanuels, she made an appointment to see them. Initially, they thought it a hoax, but when *the* Lady Diana Spencer came into their salon they realised their good fortune. She liked their work and so became a regular client. Theirs was a romantic

David and Elizabeth Emanuel in their studio in Brook Street in the heart of fashionable Mayfair, London. Their romantic style suited Lady Diana and the fairy-tale mood of the engagement and she liked their work. Soon after the engagement Lady Diana chose them to design her wedding dress, the dress of the century.

style that suited her and her temperament, exactly. This romantic theme seemed to epitomise the 'fairy-tale' atmosphere of the engagement; none could fault David Emanuel when he said, 'One needs romance in the climate in which we live. To me, if there is the excuse to dress up, you should dress up. It is very sad not to bother. And for anyone who insists on being sloppy, well she can dress down divinely.'

With hindsight, it was only natural that Lady Diana should choose the Emanuels, or someone like them, to design her wedding dress and the bridesmaids' dresses, although, at the time, this brave departure from the more traditional fashion houses, such as Hardy Amies or Norman Hartnell, caused some consternation in the ranks of the establishment.

The making of undoubtedly the most important dress of the twentieth century was a challenge that the Emanuels met head on. They began by asking the Lord Chamberlain if the dress should be bullet proof (President Reagan had been shot not that long before); but the suggestion was instantly dismissed. As the dress was of such interest, the Emanuels employed a security firm for round-the-clock protection of their salon and installed a safe. Their

Belinda Bellville and David Sassoon in their Pavilion Road salon, Knightsbridge. This partnership has been a highly successful source of both day and evening wear for the Princess of Wales since the day after her engagement when Mrs Shand Kydd introduced her daughter to Bellville Sassoon's work.

Lady Diana Spencer wearing a navy blue sailor suit made by Bellville Sassoon shortly after the engagement for the official photograph with the Queen after the Privy Council had given their consent to the marriage. This wool dress with its wide, white collar and red bow was the first in a long line of similar-style dresses.

efforts to keep the safe a secret were foiled when it stuck in the door and a crane had to deposit it through their first-floor window. Next, they found that their dustbins were being rifled. Only scraps from other work were put out and the real snippings were ceremoniously burnt at the end of each day. David Emanuel also had to go to the Royal Mews to measure up the Glass Coach which Lady Diana and Lord Spencer would take to St Paul's. He found that the coach was not large and the space for Lady Diana and her dress even more limited as 'his lordship is a big man'. The State landau that was to bring the Prince and new Princess of Wales back from St Paul's is very much larger.

While girls the world over were following the 'Lady Di look', and national newspapers were holding 'Lady Di lookalike' competitions (no men *ever* wanted to look or dress like the Prince of Wales!), the real Lady Diana was busy putting together an altogether more elegant wardrobe. At first she used just a handful of designers, those she had known or who had been recommended by her mother, her sisters or their friends at *Vogue*. They were all respected names in the fashion world, such as Bellville Sassoon, Bill Pashley, Jean Muir, Caro-

line Charles, Donald Campbell, Nettie Vogues, David Neil and Julia Fortescue, Gina Fratini, and for her hats, John Boyd.

Lady Diana began a major part of her life's task of choosing a wardrobe 'to be seen' just three days after her engagement was announced with a visit to Bellville Sassoon. This steady partnership of Belinda Bellville and David Sassoon has consistently provided the Princess of Wales with many of her most successful dresses, suits and coats from that day to the present. Belinda Bellville, whose family initially made their considerable fortune with Keen's mustard, had for some years had a dress shop in Pavilion Road, in London's Knightsbridge. Fashion was also in her family, for her grandmother, Cuckoo Leith, had a famous dress shop in the 1920s. David Sassoon was asked to join her over twenty years ago, when she had admired his designs and seen his work in his final year at the Royal College of Art. They were a perfect choice of designers in that they rarely fail to rise to the occasion by adapting their own house style, fabrics and colours to suit the Princess of Wales with the result that their creations are generally exactly right for her. They began with a sailor suit with a wide, white collar and a red bow,

ABOVE: *The eyes of the world were on the glamorous future Princess of Wales as she rode with Prince Andrew to watch Trooping the Colour, wearing a delicate blue silk dress with soft collar and matching pearl and turquoise choker. Already the public had noticed her love of bright colours and complementing jewellery.*

LEFT: *During the summer months of her engagement Lady Diana wore many pretty, flowery prints to watch her fiancé play polo. This floral-printed, cotton skirt with matching, quilted waistcoat was made by Bill Pashley. The toning lilac kid shoes were made by Alexander Gabbay of Ivory.*

first worn on the day the Privy Council held their traditional meeting to give their consent to the marriage of 'a descendant of George II'. Two years later, a pastiche of this simple suit had made it to the 'high street'.

A contemporary of David Sassoon's at the Royal College of Art was Bill Pashley, who designed and made Lady Diana's bridesmaid's dress at her sister Jane's wedding. Pashley, a tall, middle-aged Yorkshireman, works from his home in Battersea, south London. He employs no assistant, preferring to do

For the official engagement photograph taken by Lord Snowdon at Highgrove, Lady Diana wore a striking, emerald green, taffeta ballgown with elasticated sleeves made by Nettie Vogues. On this occasion she wore a spectacular diamond necklace and drop earrings borrowed from one of the royal jewellers, Collingwood.

Whenever she wears a dress in public again, the Princess of Wales is always careful to try to make it look slightly different. A few months after the wedding, a much slimmer Princess of Wales wore the same dress to a gala concert in Swansea, but this time with an emerald and diamond necklace and earrings not often seen in public.

the cutting, machining and hand-sewing himself. He starts with the fabric and his client, then he fits the design to them, rather than making the client and the fabric fit the design. As Lady Diana and then as the Princess of Wales, she kept him busy with more than a dozen creations, although not so much now as then. His creations for her are versatile, from the warm, tobacco-brown flannel suit she wore to see her amateur jockey fiancé ride at Sandown, to the delicate blue silk dress with its full collar she wore to Trooping the Colour during her engagement.' The Princess', he admitted later, 'loves strong colours like bright red.' To indulge her penchant for red, he made for her the bright red coat she wore to see Prince Charles off from Heathrow Airport on his Royal Tour of Australia.

Another occasion and another dress or suit, but such were the number of engagements, and the expense of her clothes which before her marriage were paid for by her parents, that Lady Diana was often seen wearing the same dress. She was, however, careful not to wear the same jewellery or hat, handbag or shoes so that she appeared a little different each time. For instance, for her official engagement photograph with Prince Charles, taken

by Lord Snowdon at Highgrove, she wore an emerald green taffeta evening dress designed by Graham Wren for Nettie Vogues. During the Tour of Wales, she wore the same dress to a concert in Swansea. For the Snowdon photograph, she wore borrowed diamond earrings and necklace, while at Swansea she wore her emeralds and a black velvet cloak designed by Gina Fratini.

Being only nineteen at the time of her engagement, it was only natural that Lady Diana should favour the younger designers. One such designer is Jasper Conran, highly thought of in his own right but probably more widely known as the son of Sir Terence Conran, the founder of Habitat, and his former wife, Shirley, authoress of such books as *Superwoman* and *Lace.* He has an international reputation for producing clothes that are 'cool, chic, classic and beautifully cut'. Lady Diana was wearing one such creation when she was taken by her proud fiancé to meet the people of Tetbury, the small market town close to their Gloucestershire home of Highgrove. There she wore a bright red and white, spotted wrapover jacket with a shawl collar and fitted sleeves. Like the jacket, the skirt was silk but in plain red. Many of this talented designer's clothes have been seen from then to the present day. Caroline Charles is another designer who was patronised by Lady Diana before her engagement and has continued to be so ever since. From Swindon Art School, she worked for Michael Sherard and later for Mary Quant. Setting up on her own in Beauchamp Place, London, she is no stranger to royalty, her clients including Princess Margaret and the Duchess of Kent.

By Royal Ascot, in the middle of June, Lady Diana had firmly established herself as someone guaranteed to 'steal the show' with whatever she was wearing. The Royal Meeting has always been, to the chagrin of the racing world, as much a fashion parade as a celebration of some of the finest racing in the world. During the four days she attended, the fashion-conscious and punters alike ogled the future Princess of Wales and were justifiably impressed by her choice and variety of clothes. On the first day she set herself a high standard with a predominantly mauve and yellow three-piece striped silk suit; a camisole top, blouse and skirt, which was tightly pleated to give a check effect. It came from David Neil and Julia Fortescue's salon in South Molton Street in the West End of London. Earlier in June,

she had been seen in another of their dresses (red spotted silk with bold green and blue stars frilled at the cuffs and neck) at the wedding of Prince Charles's friend, Nicholas Soames. At that time, the Neil/Fortescue partnership was not very old. After leaving St Martin's School of Art, he had worked in London and for Yves St Laurent in Paris before setting up on his own. Six years later in 1975, he was joined by Julia Fortescue, an ex-Royal College designer.

On the second day of Ascot Lady Diana was back in red. She wore a dashing red and white three-piece suit designed by Bellville Sassoon. With it, she wore a candy-striped organza blouse with full sleeves and a bold collar and bow. The skirt was slim and partially covered with a seven-eighths sleeveless coat in linen in the same shade of red. The Thursday of Ascot Week is traditionally Ladies' Day, and those who

Chosen for the beautiful cut of his clothes, Jasper Conran's first outfit for Lady Diana seen in public was the red-and-white, spotted silk jacket and red silk skirt worn for her first visit to Tetbury in May 1981. With this suit she wore a white shirt with a frilled neckline, a style for which she had already become famous.

Jasper Conran, the son of Sir Terence Conran, the founder of Habitat and of Shirley Conran, the novelist, is now well known in his own right as an international designer of high repute. As one of London's youngest designers he has created clothes for the Princess of Wales since the engagement.

attend the Royal Meeting all week tend to keep back their best for that day. For Lady Diana, it was the palest silk apricot suit designed by Benny Ong with a wrapover jacket, worn with a cream silk blouse with a pierrot collar and cream, soft, leather belt. For the final day, she chose something less exotic but nonetheless appealing – a grey and white checked dress with military buttons down the front.

No less important than the clothes, indeed essential in the Royal Enclosure at Ascot and correct for official functions elsewhere, are hats. During the engagement and since, Lady Diana went to her mother's milliner, John Boyd. Besides making most of her hats, Boyd, a softly spoken Scotsman, is unashamedly one of her greatest admirers. 'Youngsters are being led by the wrong people these days,' he said in an interview later, 'and you want to see the right sort of person giving them the lead.' To him, she

Caroline Charles in her shop in Beauchamp Place, Knightsbridge with a selection of her dashing range of highly colourful creations, which includes both day and evening wear. Lady Diana had already bought several clothes from her shop before her engagement and has continued to since then.

is 'still a wee bit of a lass'. He was trained by Aage Thaarup, the Queen Mother's milliner, before setting up on his own, with his sister.

Hats, of course, have to be worn at all official functions, and although Lady Diana was not especially fond of wearing a hat, she generally wears them to their very best advantage. Her milliners have a testing challenge when designing hats for her. A scrap of fabric and a rough sketch is generally all they have to work from. John Boyd dyes his own materials to make absolutely certain of the colour match. The edges of her veils are dyed too, often deep blue, the colour of her eyes. Among the many hats Boyd has designed for her, the Edwardian-style hat (such as she wore for Nicholas Soames's wedding) which is close fitting at the back with a large brim at the front, although not so large as to hide her face, has been one of the most successful.

In those days Boyd admitted that, 'She didn't always put her hats on properly, . . . she would come in and say, "You must be so cross with me how I put it on yesterday." But I always told her she was learning fast.'

The novelist and arbiter of good taste, Nancy Mitford, maintained that the most important item in

ABOVE: *David Neil and Julia Fortescue in their studio in London's Mayfair.*

FACING PAGE: *Never afraid to experiment with new styles and colours, Lady Diana chose for the first day of Royal Ascot a striking three-piece suit in striped silk crêpe-de-Chine, consisting of a camisole top, a blouse with softly frilled collar and cuffs and a matching narrow-pleated skirt. The outfit was designed by Neil and Fortescue, a highly successful partnership still much patronised by the Princess of Wales.*

RIGHT: *Also by Neil and Fortescue, this red-spotted, silk dress with blue and green stars was worn by Lady Diana in June 1981 to the wedding of Nicholas Soames. It was seen again nearly two years later when the Prince and Princess of Wales left Australia at the end of their long tour. The striking red hat designed by John Boyd was re-trimmed with green for the first day of the Tour of Wales in November 1981 a few months after the wedding.*

any woman's wardrobe are shoes. As Lady Diana, she bought the majority of her shoes from the better shoe shops in London, Charles Jourdan (still her only non-British supplier), The Chelsea Cobbler and Zapata, one of the 'trendier' shoe designers in London and Midas before moving on to hand-made shoes from places such as Rayne and Alexander Gabbay of Ivory, who typifies her preference for low-heeled, unfussy shoes. Later, when these flat shoes were copied, the demand was so great that one shoe factory was producing 23,000 pairs a week.

Then, as now, Lady Diana was the particular focal point of the Royal Family and, as the wedding drew closer, interest grew to fever pitch. The photographers went wild, particularly the more undisciplined of the *paparazzi*, and they pursued her at every public and private place possible. Polo, played in wide, open and semi-public parks, was an ideal sporting venue for the press to catch her as she watched her fiancé play. Tournaments and Saturday matches are less smart, sartorially, than Sunday

matches at the grander polo grounds of Smith's Lawn, Windsor or Cowdray Park in Sussex. Polo watching for her – Lady Diana (later Princess) watching for most others – generally followed a formal lunch, so she would dress for that occasion rather than for an afternoon 'by the boards' in the Royal Enclosure. These pretty summer clothes were no less smart for their casualness and had been chosen and made with the same care, usually by the same designers, as her more formal clothes. A fine

FACING PAGE: *A designer new to Lady Diana during the summer of her engagement was Benny Ong, introduced to her by Vogue's fashion editors. For Ladies' Day at Royal Ascot, always a special opportunity for ladies to show off their most stunning fashions, Lady Diana wore an apricot-coloured suit with a softly flounced, cream blouse and leather belt. With it she wore a cream, straw hat with an eye-catching arrangement of apricot-coloured flowers.*

RIGHT: *For the final day of Royal Ascot, Lady Diana wore a grey-and-white, checked dress with a military-style, double row of grey buttons down the front.*

BELOW: *Since her engagement, all but a few of the Princess of Wales's hats have been designed by a Scotsman, John Boyd. She often visits his small shop in Knightsbridge, London to discuss the success of one of his hats on a particular occasion. John Boyd is usually given only a tiny swatch of the material of a particular outfit to go by when matching or dyeing the colours.*

example is the pretty, floral-printed, cotton skirt with a matching waistcoat made by Bill Pashley. Another favourite dress on polo-watching days is her pink silk shirt dress, printed with white and blue leaves, shirred at the waist with full, elbow-length sleeves. For other events, such as Wimbledon, where she watched various matches during the two weeks of the tennis tournament, she sported a bright, printed silk suit with a wrapover jacket and shawl collar, padded shoulders and three-quarter length sleeves, a crisp white shirt and a straight skirt.

Throughout that summer of 1981, tension was mounting for *the* wedding, not least what *the* wedding dress would be like. The Emanuels' style had become well known through the media coverage, although the public did not see the two other evening dresses made by them for Lady Diana, one worn at the joint dance to celebrate the Duke of Edinburgh's sixtieth birthday and Prince Andrew's twenty-first birthday and the second worn at the ball at Buckingham Palace two days before the wedding in lieu of a wedding reception.

BELOW LEFT: *Lady Diana at the première of* For Your Eyes Only, *wearing a gold-spangled, red chiffon dress with ruched bodice. This was one of the first dresses designed for the Lady Diana Spencer by Bellville Sassoon after her engagement. With her usual care, she has matched her jewellery to the dress. Here the necklace, bracelet and earrings are of rubies and gold.*

BELOW RIGHT: *Relieved of official engagements during the weeks immediately before her wedding, Lady Diana dressed in pretty, informal clothes as she busied herself with the endless wedding preparations. For one of the wedding rehearsals she dressed in a turquoise blue, Liberty print matching skirt and shirt made from Tana lawn cotton.*

FACING PAGE: *A few days before the wedding, Lady Diana watched Prince Charles play polo at Smith's Lawn, Windsor Great Park. She is wearing the gold watch and bracelet given to her a few weeks earlier as a birthday present from Prince Charles. While Prince Charles played polo she also wore his watch for safe-keeping.*

WEDDING DAY

The day of the Royal Wedding, as the 750 million television viewers around the world and those many thousands who lined the route witnessed, was warm, sunny and bright. As the crowds gathered outside, Lady Diana woke early at Clarence House and *her* day had begun. Her mother also appeared early and mother and daughter were soon joined by David and Elizabeth Emanuel, Barbara Daly, the beautician who was to do her make-up, and Kevin Shanley, her hairdresser. Once her hair had been done and her make-up complete, she was dressed by her mother, the Emanuels and Evelyn Dagley, her lady's maid.

The hours of waiting and the months of speculation were over and the bride, Lady Diana Spencer for the last time, with her father, Earl Spencer, appeared at the gates of Clarence House. Still, as ecstatic crowds cheered every inch of the way to St Paul's Cathedral, the world had to wait to see the dress for all that could be seen through the windows of the Glass Coach were yards of the lace-trimmed train and the hint of the ivory silk bodice. However, when she stepped out of the coach, the 'secret' was out. The wedding dress was all that everyone hoped it to be, a blend of the theatrical and the romantic, a theme that echoed the mood of that fairy-tale day. As she walked up the long flight of steps of St Paul's Cathedral, the twenty-five-foot train behind her, the pale cream contrasting so vividly with the deep red of the carpet, the full effect of that beautiful dress could be seen. Made of pure ivory silk taffeta with an

Wedding Gown of The Lady Diana Spencer

The wedding dress of the Princess of Wales reflected the fairy-tale atmosphere of the occasion. The overall effect was a blend of the romantic and theatrical, a style for which the Emanuels were already famous. Their beautiful sketches show the details of the dress clearly. Made of pure silk, ivory taffeta with an over-layer of pearl-encrusted lace, the bodice had a low-frilled neckline and full sleeves gathered at the elbow. The

Carrickmacross lace had once belonged to Queen Mary and was dyed to a slightly lighter shade than the dress itself. The magnificent sweeping train was twenty-five feet long and trimmed with sparkling lace. The veil was embroidered with tiny mother-of-pearl sequins and pearls. The only jewellery worn, apart from her engagement and wedding rings, were her mother's diamond earrings and the Spencer tiara.

over-layer of pearl-encrusted lace, it had a bodice with a low, frilled neckline and full sleeves gathered at the elbow. In keeping with tradition, the bride wore something old – the Carrickmacross lace that made up the panels had once belonged to Queen Mary and had been dyed a slightly lighter shade of ivory than the dress; something new – the dress itself; something borrowed – her mother's earrings and the Spencer tiara that held the veil in place; and something blue – a tiny blue bow had been concealed in the waistband. The sweeping train was trimmed with sparkling lace and the veil was hand-embroidered with tiny pearls and mother-of-pearl sequins. Not noticed in the folds of taffeta, but nonetheless there, was a tiny, gold horseshoe studded with diamonds, for luck. Almost hidden under the full petticoats, the bride's slippers, made by Clive Shilton, were no less ornate. The silk shoes had a central heart motif made from nearly 150 pearls and 500 sequins. As a special precaution against slipping, Shilton had soled the slippers with the finest suede.

There was a slight pause at the doors of the Cathedral as the Emanuels adjusted the dress and formed up the three younger bridesmaids and two young pages. The pages wore replicas of the 1863 Royal Navy cadets' summer uniform made by Gieves and Hawkes, the top Royal Navy tailor. The three younger bridesmaids, dressed in calf-length Victorian-style flounced and scalloped dresses, wore garlands of fresh flowers in their hair and carried little baskets of flowers. Lady Sarah Armstrong-Jones, the chief bridesmaid, and India Hicks wore a

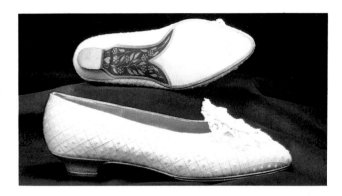

ABOVE: *The slippers worn by the Princess of Wales on her wedding day were made by Clive Shilton. They were covered in ivory silk and mother-of-pearl sequins and had a heart on the front piped in gold leather with ruffled edges, which had been personally selected by the bride. The soles were made of suede edged with gold.*

FACING PAGE: *Prince Charles greeting his bride as she arrives with her father. In keeping with tradition Lady Diana kept her veil down over her face until after the marriage ceremony had taken place. Her bouquet of fresh flowers included leaves of myrtle and veronica from bushes planted from Queen Victoria's bouquet.*

BELOW: *The seven bridesmaids and pages were dressed in styles complementing the bride and groom. The pages wore the 1863 Royal Navy cadet's summer uniform and the Victorian-style bridesmaids' dresses were made by the Emanuels. The enchanting picture was enhanced by the bridesmaids' garlands and baskets of summer flowers and their yellow sashes and shoes.*

longer version of the little bridesmaids' dresses, and they too had the yellow shoes and sash that matched the 'Mountbatten rose' (in memory of Prince Charles's 'Honorary Godfather') that was in the bride's bouquet. With those roses were white freesias, lily of the valley, stephanotis, white Odontoglossum orchids and trailing ivy leaves, and also the leaves of myrtle and veronica from bushes planted from Queen Victoria's wedding bouquet that are still growing at Osborne, on the Isle of Wight.

As the bride approached the high altar steps, the Prince of Wales turned to her and whispered, 'You look wonderful,' an undeniable statement echoed by all those lucky enough to be in the Cathedral and the millions watching on television the world over.

After the five balcony appearances, one with the famous kiss, there was a further 'treat' in store for the public, the departure for the first stage of the honeymoon. The Prince and Princess of Wales left Buckingham Palace for Waterloo Station in an open Semi-State Postilion Landau, with the Princess wearing the palest coral-pink, silk suit with a broad-frilled organza collar and short sleeves, by Bellville Sassoon. Bellville Sassoon had, in fact, made two bolero jackets, one with long sleeves in case it was cold, the other with short sleeves which was the one she wore. With it, she wore a jaunty tricorn hat of the same pink with feathers, created by John Boyd. It was a truly magical day, a day that every person who witnessed the joy and happiness of the Prince and Princess of Wales will never forget.

FACING PAGE: *The new Princess of Wales pauses to smile for photographers at the Grand Entrance in the inner quadrangle of Buckingham Palace.*

BELOW: *Huge crowds lined the route to Waterloo Station to see the Princess of Wales in her 'going-away' outfit. She did not disappoint the fashion-conscious for she wore a coral-pink suit of canteloupe silk with a bolero jacket with white organza, frilled neckline and cuffs designed by Bellville Sassoon. They had made two jackets, one with long sleeves and one with short to cope with the English weather. With the suit she wore a hat with ostrich feathers. Around her throat was a five-strand pearl choker from the 'Spencer jewellery pool'.*

HONEYMOON

Those first days of the honeymoon were spent at Broadlands, the home of the Prince of Wales's cousin, Lord Romsey, and former home of the late Lord Mountbatten. It was a grey day when they left, three days later, to fly to Gibraltar, where they were to join HMY *Britannia*. One of the most beautiful of all the wedding and honeymoon photographs of the new Princess of Wales was taken of her on the Royal Yacht, shortly before her departure. She is patently blissfully happy and looking quite lovely in her façonné crêpe-de-Chine, white skirt and jacket printed with blue and pink flowers with a blue silk camisole top. With it, she wore a blouson jacket tied casually at the waist. She had discarded the white double-breasted cashmere coat (cut in the French style) that she had worn loosely over her shoulders when she left England. The dress and jacket came from the Canadian designer Donald Campbell, who trained with John Kavanagh before setting up on his own in William Street, in Knightsbridge, London.

FACING PAGE: *For the start of the honeymoon cruise on board HMY* Britannia *at Gibraltar the Princess of Wales dressed informally in a romantic, floral-printed, façonné crêpe-de-Chine white jacket and skirt designed by Donald Campbell.*

BELOW: *The delicate jacket was softly tied at the front and underneath was a contrasting cornflower blue silk camisole top, ideal for the hot August sun of the Mediterranean. Plain white court shoes and a pearl choker completed the picture of the blissfully happy Princess of Wales.*

Campbell, who was introduced to the Princess of Wales by her sister, Lady Jane Fellowes, is another designer whom she has patronised since her engagement.

The Royal Yacht headed out into the Mediterranean, leaving squads of the press and their photographers to guess where they were going. Aboard, the Prince and Princess of Wales lived a very relaxed, but nonetheless comparatively formal life. They were accompanied by members of their Household and, as their life-style dictates, they changed for dinner every evening when they dined aboard. Although there is a full complement of officers and crew aboard HMY *Britannia*, there was still the privacy of the afterdecks for sunbathing or the occasional visit to a beach ashore where the Princess sported either a bright red or yellow bikini. Towards the end of the honeymoon, the Royal Yacht sailed into Port Said harbour, Egypt. Photographs of the occasion showed a slim Princess wearing long white cotton shorts with a wide waistband – somewhat similar to the Royal Navy white drill shorts – a white frilled shirt with puff sleeves and an open-weave straw hat. Such holiday clothes now only come out for the Prince and Princess of Wales's annual holiday to the Bahamas in February.

The designer Donald Campbell had been introduced to the Princess of Wales by her sister, Lady Jane Fellowes three months after her engagement. Since then the Princess has patronised his salon often as she finds his simple dresses in eye-catching fabrics, ranging from wool challis to delicate silk, suit her, especially for public duties.

At the end of the Mediterranean honeymoon, the Princess returned to Scotland brown and healthy. Her streaked hair, noticeably blonder, set off well her pale peach, crêpe georgette jacket and skirt from Benny Ong who is known internationally for his simple but pretty clothes and is used by the Princess of Wales today. Her shoes were plain white court, made for her by Rayne, who are also 'By Appointment' to the Queen.

With the dramatic temperature change from the Red Sea to the Highlands of Scotland, the Princess of Wales dressed accordingly. Everyday wear at Balmoral is practical, tidy but not especially smart. However, the Prince and Princess of Wales did dress up for their photocall, Prince Charles in his Royal Hunting Stewart kilt and she in a brown and white hound's-tooth suit. It was a fine creation from Bill Pashley with a loose-fitting blouson jacket which had a low waistline and an A-line kick pleat to the front and back of the straight skirt. An important event in the Balmoral summer holiday programme is the Braemar Gathering, a colourful spectacle of Highland games and Scottish country dancing. On that occasion, the Princess of Wales, to the delight of the Scottish crowd, wore a red and black plaid wool and cotton dress designed by Caroline Charles. With it, she wore a black velvet tam o' shanter.

Craithie Church, where the Royal Family worship on Sundays, always draws a large crowd. That year, the crowds were even larger to see the Princess of Wales. They were not disappointed, as each Sunday she arrived wearing something new and exciting, such as the fawn wool coat worn with a pink silk shirt and a wide-brimmed felt hat.

As with all holidays, they are over too quickly and it is back to work, even for the Royal Family. When the Princess of Wales went south in October for the start of the Tour of Wales, she was distinctly nervous of the great ordeal ahead of her. Where she might have had self-doubt, with hindsight totally unnecessary, she was at least confident in her wardrobe. As the fiancée of the Prince of Wales, she had set herself an incredibly high standard, not least in her taste and choice of clothes. As Princess of Wales, she has exceeded all expectations.

FACING PAGE: *At the end of the cruise the Princess of Wales looked tanned and relaxed. To fly back to Scotland she adapted a Benny Ong suit that she had worn a short time before at Royal Ascot, this time wearing it without the cream blouse and leather belt. She chose, instead, a soft tie belt made of the same fabric as the suit and her favourite style of shoes – plain, white court shoes – this time by Rayne, the Queen's shoemakers.*

RIGHT: *To attend the Royal Braemar Gathering the Princess of Wales chose what has since become a favourite dress of hers, especially when north of the border. Designed by Caroline Charles, it was made of red and black plaid wool and cotton piped with black Russian braid.*

ABOVE: *For the photocall by the Brig o' Dee at Balmoral the Princess of Wales wore a hound's-tooth tweed blouson jacket and skirt by Bill Pashley, well complementing her husband's choice of a kilt in Royal Hunting Stewart tartan. Her simple pair of flat leather pumps from The Chelsea Cobbler showed off her bare, suntanned legs.*

43

PUBLIC LIFE

When a member of the Royal Family arrives at an official function, anywhere in the world, he or she appears on time, unruffled and well prepared. Such organisation is down to each individual member and his or her efficient Household. As they step out of their car or off a boat or aeroplane, their effortless ease belies their true feelings. After years of practice, the Queen still has 'butterflies' at some of her engagements. The precise arrival of a member of the Royal Family also belies the exacting planning that goes into each visit. Royal tours and visits are organised in minute detail, sometimes years ahead, although the engagements at home are planned up to only six months ahead. Not least in that planning is the question of 'what to wear'.

For the male members of the Royal Family, their dress is generally straightforward and preordained. However, with all their different uniforms, their valets have no easy task, such as marrying up the right shoes with the right uniform. The female members of the Royal Family have the hardest task of all, unless they are wearing uniform. With her love of fashion, that task is one of the Princess of Wales's pleasures.

At the planning meetings, the Princess of Wales will discuss each engagement in turn. The 'committee' meets regularly at the Prince of Wales's offices, now in the semi-basement of Kensington Palace, and consists of her ladies-in-waiting, equerries and various secretaries. There, they go through the multitude of requests for her presence and match them with the Royal Tours already planned and those engagements of the Prince of Wales. When the diary has been agreed, the details of each venue will be discussed. They will try to guess at the weather not always easy in Britain, taking into consideration the time of year and the geographical position. The venue will have been seen beforehand and the clothes needed assessed; for instance, if it is likely to be windy, a smaller or closer-fitting hat will be needed. Also, the Princess of Wales has to be comfortable, neither too hot nor too cold. The nature of the engagement has to be scrutinised carefully with a style and colour to match. She has to know if she will be expected to wear a coat or overalls, put on a hat or don a miner's helmet. If so, she cannot have anything that is too full or wear a colour that will clash. She has to know exactly whom she will meet and what they will be wearing, such as a lord mayor in his scarlet livery, or the colour of a regimental uniform. Her ladies-in-waiting must also take note of what she is wearing so that they do not clash with her. The actual colour is also all important. The Welsh will never forget how 'their' Princess wore their national colours on her first visit to the

FACING PAGE: *There can be few who do not admire the natural beauty and elegance of the Princess of Wales. It is her fresh approach to her clothes and her make-up that appeals to her admirers around the world and it is no wonder that her photograph on the front cover of any fashion magazine is guaranteed to boost its sales.*

The Princess of Wales accompanied by Miss Anne Beckwith-Smith, her Lady-in-Waiting. She must always be on hand during walkabouts to help carry the presents and bouquets passed to the Princess. The 'emergency kit' in her large handbag consists of safety pins, a spare pair of tights, a needle and cotton and aspirins.

Principality; neither did the red and white check dress with a red hat and belt, the national colours of Canada, go unnoticed by the Canadians on the first day of the Canadian tour, when the Prince and Princess of Wales landed at Nova Scotia. She has to wear a colour 'to be seen', to photograph well, even if bright colours are out of fashion. It is, however, a measure of her success that she can wear these colours and in no way seem out of place.

The Princess of Wales cannot be seen wearing the same clothes too often. This, too, can be difficult for her, particularly if there is a long spell of cold or exceptionally warm weather. However, now that she is undertaking Royal tours abroad, she can wear at home many of her favourites that have already been seen abroad. She fits in well with the Royal Family, who are past masters at adapting clothes so that they are not recognised the second, even third, time round. Fortunately for the Prince of Wales, who is responsible for paying for her complete wardrobe out of his income from the Duchy of Cornwall estates, she is an economical shopper – possibly her Scots blood coming to the fore. Her many clothes are also bought at near cost price from the various fashion houses she patronises.

Kevin Shanley has looked after the Princess of Wales's hair for several years. Nowadays he always visits the Princess at Kensington Palace if she is in London or he travels to the other Royal homes, such as Balmoral and on home and overseas tours as well.

The long tours abroad are obviously the most difficult to plan, particularly if one follows directly after the other – the Canadians would not have been happy if they had recognised too many of the dresses they had seen the Princess of Wales wearing in Australia or New Zealand only three weeks before-hand. She has to take a wardrobe that will cover every eventuality and to be prepared for a last-minute change. A rich variety of style and colour in her clothes is what everyone expects. She has to plan everything minutely so that one slight change does not throw the overall concept out.

Once the clothes have been chosen and made up for a Royal tour, they are delivered to her apartments at Kensington Palace. There, they are carefully hung up until it is time for them to be packed by the Princess's lady's maid, Evelyn Dagley. Evelyn was working at Buckingham Palace as a housemaid, and promotion

To start the Royal Tour of Wales, her first endurance test, the Princess chose the national colours of Wales, red and green, for her outfit. Designed by Donald Campbell, the jacket had a peplum waist and the full, green, pleated skirt was accompanied by a dark green silk blouse. Her plain red shoes came from Rayne.

to her present post came shortly before the Royal Wedding. As the Princess's wardrobe increases almost daily, so her job grows. After the clothes have been checked and double-checked, she packs them into vast waterproof trunks, each layer separated with tissue paper, each trunk carefully labelled. Her shoes and handbags are packed in a separate trunk, while her jewellery is taken separately under guard.

Another vital member of the Princess of Wales's travelling team is Kevin Shanley, her hairdresser. He has faithfully tended her hair since her schooldays when he worked at Fenwick, the Bond Street store. Originally trained at Dorothy Gray in Conduit Street, he is now a partner of Head Lines Hair and Beauty Salon in South Kensington. He is not in awe of his royal role; he still calls his client Diana. 'I go to Buckingham Palace and Balmoral,' he confided in a recent interview. 'It did seem a bit different at first, but it's just work now...no one told me what to say or what not to say, and I've appreciated that...any-way, I'm not the type to put on an act. If I was, I wouldn't be where I am today, and that should tell you something.' He calls at Kensington Palace whenever needed and goes on tour with her, where he will attend to her hair at least twice a day, sometimes more on a hectic day. On the long tour of Australia and New Zealand, he was replaced halfway through by his colleague, Richard Dalton. The Princess of Wales, in her turn, has remained loyal to Kevin Shanley. 'She likes my work,' he is proud to say. Reports that she was to move were groundless. 'I would have been more surprised if she'd changed,' was his only comment. She has even persuaded her husband to have his hair cut by him as well; so much better than her efforts with her tapestry scissors, the Prince admitted later.

The routine of the Princess of Wales is needfully strict. After she is woken, she has a bath run for her by her lady's maid, Evelyn. On days with a public engagement, Kevin Shanley arrives to attend to her hair. While she is having her hair done, which takes anything up to an hour, Evelyn puts out her day clothes. When Kevin has finished, she puts on her make-up herself. She uses as little make-up as possible preferring the natural look. However, in common with all other pretty girls who are con-tinually photographed, she comes out better with make-up and so bows to the experts' advice – such as Barbara Daly who made her up on her wedding day and for official photographs. The Princess has a simple range that includes Clinique lipstick, Boots No. 7 Marshmallow and Lillyroot Moisturising Cream and Diorissimo scent. Her nails are still short and she generally wears just a colourless nail varnish, even for the grander engagements in the evening.

With Evelyn's help, the Princess then dresses herself. There is no margin for error, everything must be perfect. A missing button, a crease or a stray thread will be picked up and amplified in the press. When it comes to fixing her hats, extra special care is needed. For those broad-brimmed hats she uses large hat-pins; for the others, pure faith or a steadying hand.

Sailor suits

The sailor suit with its distinctive white collar
has been a favourite design of the Princess of
Wales since the early days of her engagement.
A versatile style, it can be adapted for both
formal and informal occasions all the year
round. BELOW LEFT: This bright pink silk dress
with its long white collar trimmed with a bow
was worn by the Princess of Wales two months
after the birth of Prince William for the wedding of one of her former flatmates. RIGHT: This
nautical dress by Bellville Sassoon made in the
classic colour combination of navy blue, red
and white was worn several times during the
engagement. FACING PAGE LEFT: Another
version of the sailor suit was made for the tours
of Australia and Canada. This time it was in a
cool blue and white cotton with a long pink
bow. FACING PAGE RIGHT: Another informal
sailor dress worn by the Princess of Wales for
summer evenings in 1983.

The routine is repeated throughout the day every time the Princess changes. Evelyn is always there. At the end of a full day, when she returns in the early hours of the morning, Evelyn is waiting up for her. Seeing her every day, at all hours and in all moods, Evelyn is naturally very close to her Royal mistress.

The routine for the Princess of Wales for her working days at home is similar to that of a tour abroad, although the hours are often longer if she takes in more than two engagements away from London or Highgrove. At her own request, she has been taking on more and more visits, but she still has much time to devote to herself, her husband and her son. On those off-duty days, at London and at Highgrove, she is dressed smartly but no differently to any other girl of her age and background. However, the Royal Family always changes for dinner, a dinner jacket for the men, long dresses or long skirts for the ladies, even if they have dinner on a tray in front of the television. The Prince and Princess of Wales are no exception, both at Kensington Palace and at Highgrove. Their life-style is such that they invariably dine with members of their Household or have family and friends to stay for the weekend in Gloucestershire, so they would change for dinner anyway. The Princess is indeed fortunate that she is not living in an age when women spent practically the whole day changing their clothes, for breakfast, for riding, for lunch, for their afternoon entertainment, for tea and finally for dinner.

Not even the rain and the bitter chill could dampen the ardour and support for her on her first visit as Princess of Wales to that Principality, a three-day tour in October 1981. For the first day in Wales, Donald Campbell had designed for her a truly Welsh suit of wool crêpe – a fitted peplum-waisted jacket in red with a crossover front and puffed sleeves worn over a dark green silk blouse and a full, green, pleated skirt. With it, she wore red court shoes from Rayne, and a red hat trimmed with green. She had worn the same hat, made by John Boyd, at the wedding of Nicholas Soames some four months before, only without the green trimming. The next day, the intermittent rain dampened the ostrich feathers of the Princess's pale, beige hat with a full veil, and spotted her light oatmeal cashmere coat worn over a matching skirt. The wrapover coat and skirt, worn with a silk 'pie-crust' blouse, had been designed by Caroline Charles. On the last day, her burgundy velvet suit from Jaeger matched her hat from John Boyd. Her milliner had done her well with a narrow brim, edged in silk with a full ostrich feather cascading over the back. The tour was an outstanding success, not least in the fact that the Princess demonstrated her ability to wear such a wide variety of styles and colours to such effect. The Welsh loved her for it; they would have been especially pleased had they known that the red, fringed coat with yellow and blue stripes worn by the Princess of Wales to a luncheon in the City of London on the day the news was broken that she was expecting her first child, was made from Welsh wool.

50

Another mark of the Princess of Wales and her fashion is her ability to wear sombre clothes and still look chic. For the Remembrance Sunday ceremony at the Cenotaph in London, she wore a black suit by Bellville Sassoon, enlivened by a white satin blouse, large collar and bow. Although far from feeling well when she visited Chesterfield a few days later, she still managed to look her best in a fine wool challis dress printed with poppies with a white lace collar and cuffs. With that dress she wore a green loden-style cape, trimmed with black braid which was made by Bill Pashley, black court shoes and a sombrero hat.

The Princess of Wales is never afraid to experiment with her clothes, but not always to the best effect. When she opened the new Post Office in Northampton, her first solo engagement after the wedding, she wore a brown suit edged with pink and red roses with a frilled pink collar. One reporter maintained that 'She looks like somebody's aunt.' Not so the deep blue, velvet dress with tight sleeves and a white silk scarf which she wore to switch on the Christmas illuminations in Regent Street in November. Soon after and prepared for all weathers, she chose a vivid red, wool coat with a frilled shawl collar worn with a jaunty sailor hat and full, spotted veil for her visit to Guildford Cathedral in Surrey for a carol concert. Later in the snows of mid-December when she visited Gloucester Cathedral, she wore a grey Zhivago-style wool coat with puffed sleeves, grey frogging down the front and cuffs with an astrakhan collar, turned up against the cold. Other features were the matching astrakhan hat with a silk bow and her muff. Tall, highly polished burgundy boots completed the outfit to great effect, for, despite its overall grey matching the dull skies, she still managed to look bright and colourful.

The grey weather persisted throughout the winter, including Christmas Day when the Royal Family attended matins at St George's Chapel, within the walls of Windsor Castle. For that traditional service, she wore a bright turquoise wool coat, banded in green around the pockets, collar and yoke with a stylised flower and leaf motif appliquéd at the shoulder and on the pockets. With the coat, she wore a small, pill-box hat with a black bow and black gloves, but she discarded both when she wore the same coat to visit the Dick Shepherd School in Tulse Hill in south London soon afterwards.

After Christmas, the Princess of Wales began to cut back on her official engagements and, by the time she had come back from the traditional New Year's break at Sandringham at the end of January, she was approaching her fifth month of pregnancy. Her earlier day-clothes had all been made with elasticated sides to allow for expansion, but she was soon in proper maternity clothes. A favourite maternity coat that she wore often came from Bellville Sassoon. Bright cyclamen pink in colour and made of brushed wool, it was wide at the shoulders with a frilled yoke and collar. Long ties with pompons hung from the frilled neck. John Boyd had made two similar hats to go with the coat – one

FACING PAGE ABOVE: *For the second day of the Tour of Wales, the Princess of Wales wore a practical winter coat of light oatmeal-coloured cashmere designed by Caroline Charles who also made the matching skirt and cream silk shirt with frilled collar and cuffs. The wrapover coat with its shawl collar had a matching tie belt. Her pale beige hat had what were to become two very characteristic features – an eye veil and a sweep of ostrich feathers. A tactful touch, the Princess wore the badge of the Regiment of Wales whose colonel-in-chief is Prince Charles.*

FACING PAGE BELOW: *As Princess of Wales, the Princess takes a keen interest in all things connected with the Principality; one of the many coats made for her shortly after her wedding was made of fringed Welsh wool, in a striking red tweed with yellow and blue stripes.*

ABOVE: *Ever adventurous, the Princess of Wales loves to be in the forefront of fashion whenever appropriate. Wrapped up warmly against the bitter December snows to visit Gloucester Cathedral, she wore a grey, wool coat which looked most effective with its frogging and turned-up astrakhan collar, plus matching hat and large muff.*

she wore to attend a service at Westminster Abbey to celebrate the centenary of the Royal College of Music, the other for a visit to Liverpool to open a Chinese Community Centre in April 1982. Still in the north, she wore a straight, moss-green coat with a darker green velvet collar and cuffs with a gothic scroll motif around the neck and down the front. With a wide-brimmed hat trimmed in the same velvet, it was another successful Bellville Sassoon/ John Boyd partnership.

In the spring of 1982, the Princess of Wales favoured various shades of pink for her coats, such as the fringed wool coat she wore on a visit to Huddersfield in the north of England. She wore another pink coat with a mandarin collar, buttoned down the side, for her visit to the Sony factory in Bridgend in South Wales. Such was the wind on arrival, that even her small, well-anchored pink pill-box hat nearly flew off. After the visit, photographs appeared of the Princess wearing a jaunty baseball cap with SONY across the front.

Under this rich display of coats, the Princess wore simple maternity dresses that differed little in style, or indeed colour, throughout her pregnancy for official engagements or less formal occasions. These were flowing polka-dot maternity dresses of silk, frilled at the yoke and cuffs. She had many made up for her, some in blue, others in dark and light green. For the spring visit to the Isles of Scilly, part of the Duchy of Cornwall, these pretty maternity dresses could be better seen in the warm sun without a coat. However, she donned her lodenmantel for the short journey by boat to the island of Tresco. For her last daytime engagement before the birth of her baby, the Princess wore the same blue, silk, polka-dot dress to open the Albany Community Centre in southeast London. For Trooping the Colour in June, she wore a stylish, dark green maternity dress with smocking on the shoulders, full sleeves gathered to a frilled wrist, together with a matching, dark green pill-box hat with a bow and wide veil.

FACING PAGE: *For Christmas Day the Princess of Wales wore a bright turquoise wool coat banded in green around the pockets, collar and yoke and with a colourful leaf motif in appliqué. Most of her formal maternity clothes relied on details such as appliqué work and frilled necklines to provide the fashion details.*

Although well into her pregnancy in the spring of 1982 the Princess of Wales still carried out many public engagements. She, therefore, needed to have a variety of smart, elegant coats and dresses which suited both her position and condition. This pink, wool coat with a large fringed collar was a particular favourite of hers.

BELOW: *The Princess of Wales's formal maternity dresses were made up in a variety of soft colours. Many came from The Chelsea Design Company whose simple styles with interesting necklines appealed to her. This blue, silk dress was one of the Princess's favourites and looked most elegant with only a simple pearl necklace.*

The crowds at Royal Ascot were surprised, but none-theless delighted, to see the Princess of Wales for he first day of the Royal Meeting, which turned out to be just six days before the birth of Prince William. On that occasion, she wore the simplest pale pink dress with a single bow at the neck and a matching pill-box hat with a silk rosette at the side.

There were no more public engagements for the Princess of Wales until after the birth of Prince William on 21 June, but soon after, on 18 July, she attended the Falkland Islands Service at St Paul's Cathedral. Her marine-blue, polka-dot dress, bordered with black, a black hat and spotted veil and tie belt of black suede was exactly the right blend of colour for a thanksgiving service for the cessation of hostilities as well as a memorial service for those who had died in the conflict. Her holiday at Balmoral was sadly interrupted by the tragic death of Princess Grace of Monaco. The Princess of Wales had met her shortly after the announcement of her engagement, at the reception at the Guildhall and afterwards at dinner, where they had become friends. Once again, she demonstrated her special ability to wear generally unflattering colours to her advantage, for her black dress-coat with a mandarin collar worn with a black lacquered and banded straw boater and full-face veil, looked magnificent. She looked no less fine when she wore the same suit, designed by Jasper Conran, this time with a pill-box hat trimmed with a black plume and spotted veil for the Festival of Remembrance at the Royal Albert Hall and again for a service of Remembrance at the Guards Chapel at Wellington Barracks shortly afterwards, this time worn with the addition of a frilled blouse. For some inexplicable reason, she wore her poppies on her right side as opposed to the more usual left side.

By tradition, Royal mothers are given a rest from their public engagements for some time after their children are born. The Princess of Wales wanted no such privilege, although those engagements she did fulfil were generally not overtaxing and of special interest to her. For her late autumn and winter engagements, the Princess chose a variety of colours – greens, her favourite pinks and reds, browns and even grey. She wore a tightly waisted, bottle-green velvet suit with a mandarin collar, pin-tucked at the shoulder and a full, pleated skirt to visit the Royal School for the Blind in Leatherhead in Surrey, of which she is Patron. Satin in the same bottle green was used for the sash and cuffs and to trim the matching hat, with a broad band and copious bows at the back. A hint of her white frilled blouse showed at the neck and cuffs while her calf-brown shoes and bag added another colour.

State visits of foreign Royalty and presidents always bring out the best in the British, not least the members of the Royal Family who receive their guests. For the arrival of the Dutch Sovereign, Queen Beatrix and her husband Prince Claus, at the Embankment by the Houses of Parliament, the Princess of Wales returned to her favourite colour of pink. The outlines of the flowers on the bodice of the

ABOVE: *A surprise appearance at Royal Ascot only a few days before the birth of Prince William delighted the racegoers. Dressed in a charming, soft, plain pink silk dress with a single, thin bow at the neckline and a matching hat, the Princess of Wales looked the very height of elegance. On this occasion, and on many others, the Princess has shown that simple designs and colours are the most flattering ways of looking elegant during the later months of pregnancy.*

FACING PAGE: *Green was another favourite colour worn by the Princess of Wales during her pregnancy. This moss-green Bellville Sassoon coat was enhanced by the use of darker green velvet appliqué and collar and cuffs.*

Collars

From the time of her engagement one of the most noticeable features of the Princess of Wales's taste in fashion has been her love of distinctive collars which come in all shapes and sizes. BELOW: A Bellville Sassoon outfit made for the Princess during her engagement had a bold collar and bow made of large striped organza. FACING PAGE ABOVE LEFT: The Princess's maternity clothes had plenty of collar emphasis – this cyclamen pink coat had a square-shaped yoke with frilled edges and long pompons hanging from the neck. ABOVE RIGHT: Many of the Princess's dresses and suits designed by Jan Van Velden for the summer of 1983 had the strong fashion feature of a long-pointed collar, sometimes in a contrasting brilliant white. BELOW LEFT: Another Van Velden feature of 1983 was the soft wing-collar neckline which had a tab-front button and soft ties at the centre. BELOW RIGHT: This formal day dress by Bellville Sassoon had a feature that has been characteristic of the Princess for several years – the large, soft, frilled collar in white silk with a satin bow at the centre.

tightly fitted belted jacket were quilted, the sleeves were straight but gathered at the shoulder and the neck was frilled. The skirt, of matching pink silk, was full. Under the jacket, buttoned high against the November cold of the River Thames, she wore a silk blouse with a piped, double frill. Her wide-brimmed hat, also pink and securely anchored, was worn to the back of her head.

For her visit to Capital Radio, the London local radio station, the Princess switched to brown. She had chosen the lightest brown suit with a neat donkey brown velvet collar. As a departure from the frilled neck, she had substituted a striped blouse with a stock collar. Brown, and much of it, was the order of the day for her first return visit to Wales – no brown study but a study in browns. Her wool, calf-length coat-dress was indeed striking. The coat boasted a bold, single-striped check and was trimmed in donkey-brown leather at the cuffs and mandarin collar, with matching tunic-style buttons. The waist was loosely fitted, the skirt was full and flowing over her long, brown boots and for much of the time, outdoors, she wore dark brown kid gloves. The very long skirts to the coat-dresses are a particular feature of Arabella Pollen, one of the

ABOVE: *For the Princess of Wales's first Remembrance Day service she wore a black suit with a striking white silk shirt with large frilled collar and cuffs. This outfit caused a certain amount of comment due to the perhaps inappropriate use of white on a sombre occasion.*

FACING PAGE: *Pink has always been a favourite colour of the Princess of Wales. This matching top and skirt was made of silk printed with a flower motif. The flowers were quilted on the jacket which had a highly frilled neckline and straight sleeves gathered at the shoulders. A long tie belt and simple, pink hat completed the look.*

youngest of the Princess of Wales's designers. It was a practical coat, too, for it kept her warm for the first walkabout, at Aberdyfi in mid-Wales, then on to the coast at Barmouth to launch the lifeboat, RNLB *The Princess of Wales*. Stephen Jones, who had created the light brown, suede tam o' shanter on a darker brown headband complained that she had worn it back to front. On the second day of the Royal Tour, the Welsh certainly recognised her red coat striped with flecks of blue and yellow, for it was the same coat of Welsh wool worn to a luncheon at the Mansion House shortly after her first visit to the

FACING PAGE: *When the Princess of Wales finds a style that suits her well she often has it made up in several different combinations. This coat-dress designed by Arabella Pollen was in the same style as the grey and black one opposite. This time the trimmings were in brown leather with matching boots and gauntlet gloves.*

This grey, wool coat-dress was designed by Arabella Pollen, a contemporary of the Princess of Wales and her youngest designer. Although made in plain grey flannel, it looked striking with its use of contrasting black and flashes of bright red in the hat and shoes.

Principality. At Wrexham in Clwyd she wore it with a pale blue, narrow-brimmed hat with a blue veil and a bow.

The last week of November and the first week of December were particularly busy for the Princess of Wales. For her visit to south London, to the Hearsay Centre at Catford on 30 November, she wore a particularly stylish cashmere, bottle-green suit trimmed with striped light and dark green piping around the collar, down the front and round the sleeves. The sleeves were slightly gathered. For December, it was back to pinks and reds. She began with a visit to a place close to her heart – the Great Ormond Street Hospital for Sick Children. Children, staff and parents were charmed by her visit, for which she wore a smart, crushed raspberry suit with an open mandarin collar to show the pie frills of her blouse. The jacket was square cut and worn with a matching pleated skirt. For this occasion, she dispensed with a hat.

The weather was not kind for the Princess on her visit to the Midlands to the Belgrave Lodge, Coventry. There, she wore her Jaeger burgundy velvet suit with frogging and a silk shirt with a wider-frilled collar than usual. Another London hospital where her visit gave pleasure to patients and staff was the Royal Marsden. For a change, she had substituted her usual necked blouse for a plain, turquoise blouse with a side-tying handkerchief-style neck, worn that day (and again for a visit to the Royal Academy in January 1983) with a bolero top and skirt printed with a bold Indian motif. With winter truly set in, the Princess wrapped up warmly for her next two engagements, one to a south London adventure playground where she wore a striking red, cashmere, double-breasted trench-coat. The lapels, collar and cuffs were trimmed with the same black velvet that covered the buttons. A nice touch was the black velvet half-belt stitched onto the back. For her trip to the Elephant and Castle, also in south London, she revived the oatmeal-coloured, cashmere, crossover coat with wide cuffs, shawl collar and tie belt and matching skirt that she had worn for the first Tour of Wales. This time she substituted the white blouse for a pink, frilled one. The absence of a hat on these two London occasions emphasised the the informality of the two events.

To open the new Neonatal Intensive Care Unit at the University College Hospital in London, her last engagement before Christmas, the Princess of Wales returned to a slightly more formal style, a deep blue velvet suit, pin-tucked at the shoulders and with a piped mandarin collar. Another hat by John Boyd in deep blue, an extravagant ostrich feather and a full, spotted veil lightened the somewhat sombre appea-

rance of the blue velvet. The Princess also has an identical suit in bottle green that had been seen before when she visited the Royal School for the Blind. She wore the same deep blue suit again to open the International Spring Fair at the National Exhibition Centre, Birmingham. For that occasion she wore a white blouse with the famous pie-crust collar.

After the traditional Christmas holiday of the Royal Family at Windsor Castle and Sandringham, it was back to 'work' for the Princess of Wales in February 1983. For her visit to the Bristol Royal Hospital for Sick Children she chose the same bottle-

Another favourite style worn by the Princess of Wales during the winter months was a classic, double-breasted coat in a strong colour with contrasting trimmings. This red cashmere coat made by The Chelsea Design Company had black velvet lapels, collar, buttons and a fashionable half-belt stitched on the back.

This suit is another example of a style that the Princess of Wales has had made up in other colours, in this case in deep blue and in bottle-green velvet. The use of velvet gives a luxurious feel to a somewhat severe style which relies on small details such as pin tucks at the shoulder for interest.

green cashmere suit with pretty striped piping worn with a pill-box hat that she had worn to visit the Youth Aid centre at Catford the previous November. Whereas it was generally admired, one described it on this occasion as 'a badly cut air hostess outfit' which did nothing for her 'enviably slim figure'. Her hat was criticised, too, in that 'the style may have suited her former crop, but looks wrong now'. However, the children, their parents and staff were thrilled by her visit regardless of the cut of her suit.

The visit to Nightingale House, a home for elderly Jews in Wandsworth, south London, by the Princess of Wales was judged an outstanding success for, once again, she demonstrated her great gift of charming all she meets, young and old alike. For that visit, she brought out her burgundy velvet suit from Jaeger, first worn on the first Tour of Wales.

It took the Princess twenty minutes to cover just a hundred yards as she walked towards the new shopping centre that she was to open in Aylesbury in Buckinghamshire as she talked to an excited crowd. For that early March visit, she wore what has become one of her favourite suits – the bottle-green one with the mandarin collar and pin-tucked shoulders, last seen on her visit to the Royal School for the Blind.

It was at yet another visit to south London that the Princess of Wales showed off another new suit. The voluntary workers and the members of the Parchmore Methodist Church youth and community

centre at Thornton Heath were able to admire at first hand a new peacock-green, silk suit with what is by now a feature of her jackets, a mandarin collar and puffed sleeves. This was further set off by large black buttons down the side-fastening.

For the visit of the Prince and Princess of Wales to the Royal Albert Hall for a gala concert in aid of the Royal College of Music Centenary Appeal, of which Prince Charles is President, it was an encore for the pink suit that the Princess had first worn for the December visit to the Great Ormond Street Hospital for Sick Children. This time her shoes and handbag were dark blue.

Those who came to see and meet the Princess of Wales on her trip to Reading had a preview of one of her suits that she had had made for the Royal Tour of New Zealand. It was a royal blue, woollen, wrapover coat-dress trimmed in black round the mandarin collar and down the side-fastening.

Devon in March can be cold and the Princess chose her long Arabella Pollen coat-dress (the brown check one that she had first worn for her second visit to Wales). She had substituted the tam o' shanter for a jaunty brown felt trilby. As Patron of the Preschool Playgroups Association, she went to the small towns of Bovey Tracey and Tavistock to visit groups within the scheme.

These were all hectic, but nonetheless enjoyable, visits for the Princess of Wales for she knew that in a few days, on 20 March, she would be off on her first major Royal Tour of Australia and New Zealand. However, with such a daunting prospect ahead, she still had time to give her all to the job in hand, however small by comparison to what lay ahead.

On her return from the exhaustive but highly successful Royal Tour and a chance to recuperate on the Island of Eleuthera in the Bahamas, the Princess of Wales looked fit, bronzed and well. Soon after her return, it was back to the rounds of her public duties. Her first visit, always pleasurable where children are concerned, was to an adventure playground for handicapped children in Cheltenham. On that bright, sunny May day, she wore the same elegant wool challis dress printed with poppies from Donald Campbell that she had first worn for the visit to Chesterfield eighteen months earlier.

June is invariably a Royal month and not least in the list of royal events is Trooping the Colour to

Looking tanned after a Caribbean holiday, the Princess of Wales visited an adventure playground in Cheltenham wearing a favourite dress – a Donald Campbell design made in black wool challis printed with red and white poppies and worn with one of her distinctive blouses.

mark the Queen's official birthday. It is a time when the whole Royal Family is 'on show' to and from Horse Guards Parade, followed by the popular balcony appearances. For the 1983 ceremony, an even louder cheer went up as the ever-popular Queen Elizabeth the Queen Mother and the Princess of Wales travelled together from Buckingham Palace to Horse Guards Parade and back again in an open State Landau. They were a beautiful pair, the Queen Mother in a light pastel blue, the Princess wearing a grey silk printed two-piece by Jasper Conran. The top, softly gathered at the shoulders, was drawn in by a grey suede belt and the skirt was full and pleated. With it, she wore a grey straw boater with matching handbag and shoes. The whole outfit was to be seen again on the tour of Canada.

After the tour of Canada, the Prince and Princess of Wales had just a month before the start of their Scottish holiday. They had both worked hard on their two Royal Tours and their engagements were kept to a minimum. There were, however, engagements that the Princess did not want to miss such as the luncheon organised by the Variety Club of Great Britain. Wearing the same dress, the fuchsia and white, spotted dress by Donald Campbell that she wore at Fremantle on the Australian tour, she spent a happy afternoon with an enthusiastic and colourful crowd which included 300 handicapped children.

Holidays at Balmoral for the Royal Family are not all relaxation for it is an admirable chance to undertake local, and not so local, Scottish engagements. One such visit for the Princess of Wales was to the Keiller sweet factory in Dundee. This engagement caused even more interest than usual after the rumours that she was pregnant. However, she was giving no secrets away when she donned a white coat and trilby over a favourite number of hers, the Scottish plaid dress with white collar and cuffs by Caroline Charles.

The Princess of Wales wore another 'favourite' in the form of the red, striped, Welsh wool coat to visit the disabled servicemen at the Erskine Hospital, just outside Glasgow at the beginning of September. She was to return to Glasgow a week later, 10 September, to visit Coatbridge, not far from the city. On that occasion, she wore, for the first time in public, a stylish, grey wool dress with full sleeves cuffed with twin buttons, a round white collar and white bow. Again the visit caused a stir with the speculation of her pregnancy. At one point, she cleverly avoided the photographers who tried to photograph her examining baby cots made by workers on the Youth Employment Scheme.

Throughout the autumn and early winter, the Princess of Wales carried out a few local engagements, such as visits to playgroups in south London where she wore some of her dresses and suits last seen on the two Royal Tours. However, in early October, she wore a favourite from the past, the pretty coral-pink silk 'going away outfit' to open the new District General Hospital in Grimsby. For this occasion, she wore the jacket with the shorter sleeves.

The day-to-day engagements of the Prince and Princess of Wales receive only national interest, unless something untoward happens or it surrounds a controversial or personal event. An overseas tour attracts a little more international interest, but the latest Royal Tours of Australia, New Zealand and afterwards, Canada, by the Prince and Princess of Wales made headline news throughout the world. Inevitably, part of this interest in Australia and New Zealand was because of Prince William who was 'on show' for the first time, part was the popularity of both the Prince and Princess of Wales and, inevitably, part was due to the variety of the Princess's wardrobe that rarely failed to complement her and delight her admirers.

From the day of her wedding the Princess of Wales has dazzled Britain and the world with her fashion sense, but the hugely successful Royal Tour of Australia and New Zealand was a turning point. For the first time it seemed that the Princess of Wales was truly self-confident in expressing her personality, never putting a foot wrong. Not even the most obstinate Australian republican seemed able to resist the Princess and that means that the image she projected was the right one – proud, happy and flamboyant. This was no lucky accident but the reward of months of planning. Above all, despite all the advice poured upon her, it was the Princess herself who decided what to wear and when.

In the first place there was the Australian climate and the landscape to consider. One moment she would be in the strange and empty outback, the next, at a formal city dinner or in a small town in the middle of nowhere. Her clothes had to be flexible and comfortable to wear. In the heat, the Princess needed to be informal to avoid looking overdressed as perhaps the Queen did on her recent visit to Kenya. As a young woman she needed to ensure that the role of Princess made sense in the most unpompous of societies. Her dayclothes had an almost boyish look which was quite appropriate to the great, wide, open spaces of Australia.

The Australians, of course, also enjoy glamour with a capital G and it was important not to disappoint them. Perhaps a Princess in Australia was an anachronism but if so, then it was a role not to be ashamed of but to flaunt. So we saw the Princess of Wales, even in small towns, creating a delightful sense of almost incongruous glitter by dressing in the finest silks and in the most audacious designs.

This was a new audience, to be wooed and won and the Princess triumphantly achieved her object. In a land in which elegant dress and fine materials can seem absurd or at least inappropriate, she created a new vivid style, modern and young with a

In the heat of central Australia, the Princess of Wales always looked fresh and comfortable yet distinctive enough to stand out in a crowd. This bright, yellow and white silk dress was worn with a plain, white, leather belt and hat with plain white shoes and bag.

For the arrival in Australia, the Princess of Wales wore a Jan Van Velden dress of turquoise silk with a distinctive, large, pointed collar. The top had long pin tucks as far as the hips and a soft, pleated cummerbund at the waist. These Van Velden features were to be seen again on several other dresses during the tour.

hint of practicality during the day and in the evening dazzling and dignified. The tour began in the very heart of Australia, when their Royal Australian Airforce Boeing landed at Alice Springs. It was a relaxed and confident Princess of Wales who stepped onto the tarmac. Her hairdresser, Kevin Shanley, had put the final touches to her hair and she had recently changed into the first of many different day dresses and suits that were to be seen during the tour that was to last for forty-one days and forty nights. For her arrival she chose an eau de Nil calf-length dress with a striking pointed collar. The full half-sleeves were buttoned just above the elbow and the shirt-waisted top was pin-tucked as far as the hips and drawn in at the waist with a matching, pleated cummerbund. It was designed by Jan Van Velden, a Dutchman who has been working in England for many years. His hallmark is his ability to produce 'strikingly pretty, feminine clothes' such as the sunshine yellow, silk dress with a stylised white flower motif she wore for the first engagement to visit the Alice Springs School of the Air. The dress, with its full, gathered skirt, was somewhat reminiscent of a man's evening shirt. The soft wing collar stood up from the pleated front with long ties in a bow at the neck. This dress, worn with a broad, white, leather belt, handbag and low court shoes, suited her well and was a perfect foil for her fair hair.

At sunset the next day, 21 March, the Prince and Princess of Wales went to the awesome Ayer's Rock, the mystical centre of the Aborigines' world. Despite the strong sun, the Princess did not wear a hat with her white cotton Jacquard dress. Designed by Benny Ong, it was a button-through dress with a boat-shaped neck and elbow-length sleeves, clinched tightly at the waist by the now familiar broad leather belt with a matching shoulder bag. Forewarned, she wore tan, flat-soled pumps trimmed in white to climb part of the way up the deep red, sandstone face of the rock. The final adornment to her dress was a badge saying 'I climbed Ayer's Rock'. Benny Ong also designed the two-piece for her next engagement – a visit to Karguru School, three hundred miles from Alice Springs. It was hot, but the Princess managed to look cool in the crêpe-de-Chine, ivory shirt-waisted top and pale mint-green skirt. It was an informal affair and no one was surprised that she was bare legged and, again, wore no hat. Lunch with the new Prime Minister, Robert Hawke, and his wife at their official residence, The Lodge, was, however, a formal affair and the Princess dressed accordingly. She had chosen a turquoise suit from The Chelsea Design Company. It was in a style that particularly suited her. The jacket with its mandarin collar was pin-tucked at the front and tightly sashed at the waist with a pretty bow, the semi-full sleeves drawn in at the wrist with frilled cuffs. The matching skirt was her usual calf-length and the suit was worn with a matching rouleau hat and veil from John Boyd.

Those close followers of the Princess's fashion might have recognised the pale pink suit with the matching hat and its jaunty feathers that she wore for the second day in Canberra. It had been seen before as she left Buckingham Palace for Waterloo Station for the start of her honeymoon on the day of the Royal Wedding. On that occasion she had worn the short-sleeved jacket while for the visit to the Australian capital she wore the longer-sleeved version for protection against the scorching sun.

An unscheduled trip on the tour was a visit to Cockatoo, the scene of the terrible bush fires which were dangerously close to Melbourne. During World War Two, the Queen (the present Queen Elizabeth the Queen Mother) was always careful to choose exactly the right clothes when she visited blitzed areas of Britain, maintaining that 'If they came to see me, they would wear their best clothes'. On the same premise, the Princess was careful not to 'dress down' for the tragic scene, where so many had lost their lives or all their worldly possessions. For the stricken inhabitants of Cockatoo, she wore an elaborate dress from Gina Fratini. The multicoloured candy-striped silk dress was typical of the designer with its frilled neck and matching frills on the yoke, front and back.

Another new designer whose work had been seen, and admired before, was the young Arabella Pollen.

She designed the blue, cotton sailor dress with two white panels down each side that the Princess wore to visit Stirling. The dress had a white sailor collar and a pretty, long, pink bow. Light blue, circular cuff links held the white cuffs below full sleeves. Arabella Pollen, then just twenty-one, is the youngest of the Princess's designers and also her closest in age. It is thus not surprising that, with her adventurous spirit the Princess of Wales should try a talented contemporary.

Another dress designed by Bellville Sassoon was worn by the Princess for a daytime visit to the Sydney Opera House and later to lunch at Parliament House, the unfinished building of the New South Wales legislature. The pink, silk crêpe-de-Chine dress, with printed white daisies and pale blue stalks and a matching battledress jacket, tied at the waist, softly gathered at the shoulders and cuffed above the elbow, had been seen before as it was the dress that she had worn for the christening of Prince William.

As the Prince and Princess of Wales arrived for their short visit to Newcastle on 29 March, an announcement went out over the loudspeaker system to the 43,000 children in the stadium: 'We all

There was also a more formal side to the Australian tour and the Princess of Wales dressed accordingly. For lunch with the Prime Minister, she wore an elegant, turquoise, silk suit. The jacket had a mandarin collar and pin tucks down the front and was tightly sashed at the waist with a pretty bow. The cuffs were softly frilled.

For the second day in Canberra the Princess of Wales wore her going-away outfit made by Bellville Sassoon in canteloupe silk with white organza collar and cuffs. This time she wore the jacket with long sleeves to protect her arms against the scorching sun.

want to see you wave to the Prince and Princess, and I'm sure the beautiful Princess Diana would like to see you wave too.' Indeed she did. For that occasion, she wore the palest of rose-pink dresses, a colour she has tried and tested so often and one that she knows suits her so well. The candy-striped silk dress from

The Chelsea Design Company was worn with a short, blouson, wrapover jacket in plain silk with a tricorn hat by John Boyd.

Another outfit that had been seen two summers before was the striking dress, blouse and coat worn by the Princess of Wales for the first day of their two-day visit to Tasmania, beginning in the island's capital, Hobart. The outfit had been designed by Bellville Sassoon, originally for the second day of Ascot, nearly two years before. For the second day on Tasmania, she wore a white gabardine suit by Jasper Conran and a close-fitting hat with pale gardenias

and spotted veil of the same colour from John Boyd. The narrowness of the hip-length coat and the slim skirt accentuated her own slim figure, while the simplicity of the style and colour was well set off by bright red shoes and handbag.

Back on the mainland of Australia, the Prince and Princess were reunited with their son, Prince William, who had been staying at Woomargama, near Albury. For Matins on Easter Day, the Princess mixed her designers, although not her colours. Her turquoise dress, the same as for her arrival at Alice Springs, from Jan Van Velden's salon, was worn with a quilted, flowered jacket from Miss Antonette, bought 'off the peg' from Harrods. It was a good

LEFT: *For an informal visit to Stirling, the Princess of Wales wore a favourite style, a sailor suit in blue and white cotton made by Arabella Pollen. Striking features included the long, pink bow and circular, blue cuff links to hold the white cuffs together at the wrist.*

FACING PAGE: *The Princess of Wales makes good use of her wardrobe, often wearing her favourite outfits on several occasions. She had worn this pink, floral-printed, silk dress and jacket with elbow-length sleeves for the christening of Prince William nine months earlier.*

BELOW: *For the visit to the cooler climate of Hobart in Tasmania, the Princess of Wales wore the Bellville Sassoon suit she had worn at Royal Ascot shortly before her wedding; the slim skirt and sleeveless coat were in a dashing red with a candy-striped, organza blouse.*

BELOW: *This classic, Jasper Conran suit in white gabardine shows the Princess of Wales's dashing use of colour. The simplicity of the design and the colour, a well-known feature of Jasper Conran's style, was well set off by the bright red shoes and handbag.*

match, the turquoise braid and large buttons of the quilted, Chinese-style jacket and the John Boyd turquoise straw hat with a wide brim and silk band that fell down her back disguising the dress so well.

Rest time over, the Royal Tour continued in Adelaide. As the capital city of Southern Australia, the Princess dressed in a more formal style for the visit to the Parks Community Centre. She chose a two-piece suit by Arabella Pollen; predominantly cream, it had pyjama stripes worn over a silk blouse with a narrow, pierrot collar. The skirt was long, a feature of Miss Pollen's style. It was, indeed, a contrast to her other clothes of the tour which, in general, flattered her figure: this suit, from a young designer, was surprisingly matronly. At the University that night, the mood was less formal and the Princess dressed accordingly for a dance exclusively for the 'under forties'. She wore a Jan Van Velden creation, a calf-length, black, silk skirt with a white blouse printed with heavy, black brush-strokes all over and with characteristically full sleeves drawn in at the elbow. To finish off, she wore a black leather belt tied at the front and a striking pair of black and white peep-toed court shoes with striped insets.

The soft pastels of the previous engagements were soon overtaken by the bright red that is so often

Here the Princess of Wales shows the versatility of many of her clothes. On the facing page she wears the same Jan Van Velden dress worn for the arrival in Australia but this time, as she was attending church on Easter Sunday, she wore a pretty, quilted jacket on top and a straw hat trimmed in silk. Later on in the tour she wore the same flowery jacket but this time with its matching skirt and a hat she had worn earlier on in Canberra.

associated with the Princess of Wales. To visit Renmark and Port Pirie she wore another of Jan Van Velden's suits. The red of the full-yoked jacket was accentuated by the white, pointed collar and fringed waist in the same style as the turquoise dress of her arrival in Australia. The suit was set off by a fetching white straw hat trimmed in a matching red, red shoes and red handbag. Another venue and another shade of red. For the visits to Fremantle, a solo engagement to open the Princess of Wales Wing of the hospital, and to Perth, she chose a pretty, pink, silk dress spotted with white. Donald Campbell had designed the wrapover dress with its soft, wide cummerbund, tight sleeves and slim skirt and John Boyd the matching pill-box hat with a flamboyant bow. Later that same day she changed into a blue, silk dress from The Chelsea Design Company. The dress, with its blouson sailor jacket and white bow, had a square neck and calf-length skirt, both banded in white.

Nearing the end of their exhaustive tour, the Royal couple visited the town of Bunbury. For this visit, the Princess wore a Caroline Charles suit, of silver-grey silk printed with white butterflies and worn with a silk blouse with a sailor collar, tied softly at the front. The suit was well set off by a red cummerbund. After two days of rest, the Prince and Princess attended the tiny church of St Paul, Holbrook. The suit she wore for Holy Communion, a striped three-piece from Neil and Fortescue, was the same worn at Royal Ascot two years earlier, before her wedding.

Brisbane, the capital of Queensland, gave such an enthusiastic welcome to the Prince and Princess of Wales that there was a serious danger of their being trampled by the crowd as they walked up to the City Hall. The heat was intense, too, but the Princess managed to stay calm and cool. On that occasion, she wore a clever silk dress by Donald Campbell. Predominantly white with printed blue flowers, it had a cross panel on the left-hand side with reverse printing as did the tie belt.

With so many occasions to cater for, the Princess and her advisers had cleverly thought out how her wardrobe could be put together in various combinations. Shoes and handbags were easy but hats were more difficult. However, she did manage the occasional switch, such as the white straw hat trimmed with red which she wore at Port Pirie and which went well later on with the dress and jacket she wore at Altona and Melbourne. Bought from The Chelsea Design Company, this silk dress was white with bold red spots with a round neck and a full skirt; the jacket was in the same red with half sleeves and trimmed round the edges with wide, white silk braid. Another combination was worn on the first day of their visit to Melbourne, including a trip to Sovereign Hill, a preserved eighteenth-century village. For this, she wore the 'off the peg' suit by Miss Antonette, (the same jacket had been worn with a dress at Albury for church on the first Sunday of the tour). Still in Melbourne, the Princess wore another dress that had been seen in England two

Hats

When the Princess of Wales is on an official engagement she usually wears a hat, the majority being made by John Boyd. RIGHT: This jaunty pink hat with ostrich feathers was worn by the Princess of Wales with her going-away outfit. BELOW: Most of the Princess's hats, such as this one, are small and worn off the face so that the crowds can see as much of her as possible. FACING PAGE ABOVE LEFT: Stephen Jones designed this soft beret made in light brown suede with a darker brown headband. The design was also made up in black and red (see page 61). ABOVE RIGHT: The Princess's milliners must always remember that her hats must look stylish from all angles. This simple design with a silk rosette has also been made in peacock green (see page 77). BELOW: A large hat worn by the Princess on her 22nd birthday for the final day of the Tour of Canada.

The designers who work for the Princess of Wales have to remember always that her clothes must look as stylish from the back view as from the front. This Donald Campbell, pink-and-white spotted silk dress had a soft wide cummerbund and a lovely row of matching buttons down the back. The matching pink John Boyd hat with its flamboyant bow looked just as striking from the back as it did from the sides and the front.

years previously. This was the red, silk, polka-dot dress with green and blue stars, frilled at the neck and the cuffs, which she had worn to Nicholas Soames's wedding. On that occasion she had worn a red, wide-brimmed straw hat, but to leave Australia after their highly successful tour she wore another wide-brimmed hat of cornflower blue, the side stitched to the crown reminiscent of a bush ranger hat worn by the Australian army.

During the flight from Melbourne to Auckland for the start of the Royal Tour of New Zealand, both the Prince and Princess of Wales had plenty of time to change. The Princess was well prepared for the cold and drizzle, a feature that was to persist throughout their tour of the two islands, when she stepped out of the aeroplane dressed in a most stylish white coat-dress trimmed with tan around the wide collar and the cuffs from The Chelsea Design Company. Made of the finest wool, the bodice was close fitting, the sleeves gathered at the shoulder and the skirt full. Her pill-box hat was also white, trimmed with a light brown band, silk bow and spotted veil.

The rain cleared for the Prince and Princess's first meeting with the inhabitants of Auckland, when they drove round the Eden Park sports stadium, standing in the back of an open Rolls Royce. The 35,000 cheering children had a splendid view of them both. For this occasion, the Princess had chosen an interesting green dress designed by Donald Cambell. Like the blue and white dress of his she had worn in Brisbane, this silk dress was an equal blend of green and white stripes and green with white polka-dots cut to exactly the same style as the blue version. The brightness of the green was accentuated by her white hat with a turned-up brim with a fluffy ostrich feather at the back. As the tour continued, so did the rain. Those who had come many miles to see the Royal couple were disappointed that they could not see more of the very pretty, yellow, silk coat-dress, as it was hidden by her fawn mackintosh. Her matching straw boater trimmed with a cream band, a bow and a flower was also partially hidden under an umbrella. The coat-dress, from the Chelsea Design Company, was frilled at the neck and cuffs and buttoned down the front.

Another Jan Van Velden variation of a silk dress that the Princess had worn twice before in Australia, the yellow and white printed dress with the pin-tucked front and wing collar, was worn for her visit to the fire-station in Manukau. This time it was a navy blue and white suit in the same pattern as the dress and worn with a white blouse in the identical style. A wide-brimmed, white hat accentuated the conservativeness of the suit. The people of

The sailor suit is an excellent style of dress for a fairly formal event in hot weather as it looks both cool and elegant. The Chelsea Design Company created this one for a garden party in Perth. Made of blue silk, it was banded in white with a matching jaunty boater trimmed in silk and a small veil.

For the damper climate of New Zealand, the Princess of Wales's first outfit was a white coat-dress from The Chelsea Design Company. With a close-fitting bodice and full skirt, it was stylishly trimmed in tan around the wide collar and cuffs and had two rows of tan buttons down the front. The hat continued the colour theme.

Wellington were especially fortunate, for not only did they see the stylish, green dress at the start of the tour, they also saw her in two other very different creations. The first was a peacock-green suit with a peplum-waisted, fitted jacket and a full skirt worn with a white, frill-neck blouse and a matching hat with a large silk rosette. For the meeting with Prince Edward, who had been in New Zealand for seven months as a tutor and housemaster at Wanganui Collegiate, the Princess sported a royal-blue, side-fastening wrapover woollen coat-dress, trimmed with black braid around the mandarin collar, the cuffs and the side edge, accompanied by white spotted tights.

Although it was not an official daytime engagement it was at least a very public one when Prince William went on his first 'crawlabout' in the grounds of Government House in Auckland. For the great occasion, his mother wore another of Jan Van Velden's dresses. It was identical in style to the

dress in which she had arrived at Alice Springs, but this time it was made of green silk spotted with white, with a large, white, silk, pointed collar. The sleeves were full and the matching full skirt had side-buttoning. The next day, for a garden party at Government House, the Princess wore the same white blouse with black splashes that she had worn in Adelaide. However, for the garden party she added a white straw hat with a wide silk band in black with a full bow at the back, and substituted a white skirt for the black one she wore at Adelaide. She also wore a single red poppy then, and again for the service held the next day to commemorate ANZAC Day. Dressed suitably for the occasion, the Princess wore a simple, grey, wool coat-dress with a mandarin collar trimmed in the lighter dove grey and a grey pill-box hat with a white band and black and white ostrich feathers.

The tour continued and the next day the Royal Party watched an aerobatic display, the Princess wrapped up against the cold in the oatmeal, cashmere coat, matching skirt and blouse which she had worn for the second day of the tour of Wales. For the last day of the tour, a visit to a gathering of Maoris on the Bay of Islands, the Princess kept back one of the most spectacular of her extensive wardrobe. It was a bright yellow, high-necked, silk suit from The Chelsea Design Company. That particular shade of yellow does suit her so well, especially when her hair is lightened by the sun. The short jacket was quilted and side-buttoned with a square collar to show the mandarin collar of the matching silk blouse below. The matching skirt was pleated from a narrow waistband. The close-fitting hat had a medieval rouleau band and veil.

As the Prince and Princess of Wales boarded the RAF Boeing on 30 April, their tour had lasted for forty whole days and, apart from the few days of relaxation, they were 'on view' and working solidly throughout. It was a triumph of stamina for them both, of organisation by their Household and, not least, of the success of the Princess's designers to match her own beauty and shining personality with their clothes.

These two dresses from Donald Campbell show his clever use of contrasting prints. The green dress made for the cooler climate of Auckland in New Zealand, had long sleeves but in every other respect the styles were identical. The green dress used the theme of thin white stripes and polka-dots repeated in the soft tie belt at the waist.

The blue dress worn in the heat of Brisbane had shorter sleeves and the theme of floral prints, white flowers on a deep blue background and vice versa. The simple style of these dresses emphasised the clever reversing of the prints. On both occasions white was the colour used for the accompanying hat, shoes and bag.

This suit designed by The Chelsea Design Company was one of the few of the new outfits made for the Tour of Australia and New Zealand to be seen in England beforehand. With her slim figure, the Princess of Wales can wear peplum-waisted jackets successfully. The matching hat had an enormous rosette on one side.

Another bright colour often worn by the Princess of Wales is royal blue. This wrapover, woollen coat-dress, with its contrasting black trim on the collar and cuffs and also down one side, was a cheerful note on an overcast day when the Prince and Princess of Wales visited Prince Edward at Wanganui Collegiate.

Hardly had the Prince and Princess of Wales returned from the other side of the world than they were off again in June, across the Atlantic for their eighteen-day Royal Tour of Canada. It is not unfair to say that the Canadian Tour was not the popular success that the Australian tour had been. Australia had been the Prince of Wales introducing his Princess to an old flame – she might have hesitated or become flustered. But in her style and bearing, in the primary colours she favoured, the Princess was self-confidence itself. She seemed to fall in love with Australia and New Zealand and they with her.

Canada, as it turned out, was a greater challenge – a more sophisticated society perhaps than Australia and less ready to be overwhelmed by a fashion-conscious princess. Again, as in Australia and New Zealand, there was the sophisticated use of primary colours. She favoured the checks, polka-dots and bold stripes that can make one look like a not very attractive national flag but with a clever designer has the cheekiness of the musical chorus. Her sailor suits were again typical of the boyish look the Princess can use so effectively. Indeed, the theatrical element in her clothes on this tour seemed to be deliberate and

ABOVE: *For the informal photocall in Auckland the Princess of Wales wore another Jan Van Velden dress. The long-pointed collar had become a favourite feature by now. It was repeated this time in brilliant white which contrasted well with the rest of the dress made of green and white spotted silk.*

FACING PAGE: *For the last engagement in New Zealand the Princess of Wales wore one of her most spectacular outfits. Made by The Chelsea Design Company, it was in bright yellow silk with a short, quilted jacket which was fastened at one side by large buttons. The Princess is wearing a lucky charm presented to her by the Maoris.*

just right. To be principal boy in the pantomime and be fairy princess was a wonderful combination.

In common with everywhere they go, there was a tremendous welcome as they landed at the Sheer-water Airforce Base at Halifax, Nova Scotia. No Canadian can have failed to notice that the Princess of Wales was wearing the national colours of red and white. Her dress was white with a deep red check, with full sleeves and a high mandarin collar. The dress, with its pleated front, was side-fastened and enlivened at the neck by a large bow. Extra splashes of colour were the deep red belt, handbag and hat. The next day, when they visited the Royal Canadian

ABOVE: *Another outfit worn in Canada which had been seen already in New Zealand was the striking pale yellow, silk coat-dress from The Chelsea Design Company. Its features included many of the Princess's favourites such as the drop waist, the double-breasted front with two rows of buttons and softly frilled neckline.*

For meeting the Mic Mac Indians in Canada the Princess of Wales wore the navy blue and white suit which had been seen before in New Zealand. The suit was typical of Jan Van Velden with the pin-tucked front and wing collar. The abstract print was the same pattern as that used on the yellow and white dress worn in Alice Springs.

FACING PAGE: *For the arrival in Canada the Princess of Wales chose deliberately to wear the national colours of red and white. The deep red and white check dress had a pleated front and a large bow at the neck. The same deep red was repeated for the accessories of handbag, belt and stylish hat.*

Dockyard Ship Repair Unit at Halifax, she wore the same chic white and tan coat that she had worn for her arrival in New Zealand. It rained for part of the visit and the Princess had to wear her mackintosh.

The bright red of her wool suit and black sombrero hat, worn for the visit to the United Empire Loyalists at Shelburne, Nova Scotia was another thoughtful touch seen in her Canadian wardrobe for it perfectly matched the uniforms of the Royal Canadian Mounted Police. The three-quarter length jacket with matching straight skirt was worn with a polka-dot white silk shirt with a pussy cat bow at the neck. Another pretty dress which had been seen on the tour of New Zealand was the frilled yellow coat-dress from The Chelsea Design Company that she wore at St John, for the beginning of the tour of New Brunswick on the mainland. The navy-blue suit with the stylised, white motif and white blouse with its wing collar which she wore to meet the Indian chiefs of the Mic Mac tribe at Charlo had also been seen on the tour of New Zealand. Still in New Brunswick, it was a chill and misty morning that saw the Royal Barge from the HMY *Britannia* bring the Prince and Princess of Wales to Matins at All Saints' Church at St Andrews-by-Sea. Almost as a foil to that grey, swirling mist, the Princess came ashore in a white suit. The suit, worn with a silk blouse with a pierrot collar, was beautifully tailored by Jasper Conran.

For the arrival of the Princess of Wales to Ottawa, the capital city of Canada, the Princess chose a particularly striking dress of white silk with bold,

Another example of a striking Donald Campbell print was worn by the Princess of Wales for the visit to the Canadian capital, Ottawa. Made of white silk with bold blue and narrow yellow stripes, it had a square neckline and covered buttons down the front, finishing in a soft cummerbund of the same material.

Another dress that was seen in both Australia and Canada was the pink, candy-striped dress worn with a plain silk, short jacket. This is a colour that the Princess has tested on many occasions. The longer hems that she favours are not just fashionable but are a practical necessity for occasions such as tree-planting.

Eye veils

Shortly before her marriage Lady Diana Spencer appeared in a jaunty hat with a striking eye veil (see page 24). This was the first in a long line of hats to use veiling as a way of decorating a simple style. John Boyd, her favourite milliner, uses real silk veiling which is difficult to obtain. Working from a small swatch of the fabric being used for the main outfit, he uses cold-water dyes to achieve a perfect match for the hat-base, the veiling and other trimmings. RIGHT: A striking yellow veil. BELOW LEFT AND FACING PAGE BELOW: The same design has been used for both hat-bases but they were made up in different colours and pattern of veiling. BELOW RIGHT: The deep blue of this full veil matches perfectly the colour of the Princess's eyes. FACING PAGE ABOVE: The overall white of the suit and hat was enhanced by the subtle use of pale tan.

blue and narrow yellow stripes, square neck and long sleeves and drawn together with a wide cummerbund of the same material. It was Arabella Pollen's light blue, cotton sailor dress, first worn in Australia, which came out again for the informal barbecue at Kingsmere Farm, not far from Ottawa. Another dress from the Australian tour which appeared again was the pink, candy-striped dress with a plain silk jacket from The Chelsea Design Company which the Princess of Wales wore to meet the people of St John's, Newfoundland. The next day for their second day in Newfoundland, she revived another creation of The Chelsea Design Company that she had worn in Australia, the white dress with the large, bright red spots and the red jacket.

Strong colours were the order for the next two days' engagements, an especially striking emerald-green suit for the 400th centenary celebrations of St John's. With it, she wore a white silk blouse with a mandarin collar and a tricorn hat. On the last day in Newfoundland, she wore a cobalt blue, cashmere coat, the buttons, collar, pockets and cuffs trimmed in black. With it she wore a black and white polka-dot blouse, the ties well tucked in, and the same black sombrero hat as worn in Shelburne at the beginning of the tour.

The sailor dresses had become very much part of the Princess's wardrobe. For her visit to Charlotte-town, she had chosen a particularly stylish variation. This one was in lilac grey with a dropped waist and a pleated skirt with a white, silk, scalloped sailor collar. It was back to pink again for her visit to Montague and the raspberry pink suit with the side-buttoning jacket and pleated skirt first worn at home for her visit to the Great Ormond Street Hospital for Sick Children the previous December. In Canada, she substituted the frilled blouse for a simpler one with a straight, stand-up collar. Yellow is another colour that suits the Princess, particularly for hats. The bowler-style hat with a fluffy ostrich feather from her milliner, John Boyd, was a contrived match with the silk collar, cuffs, covered buttons and piping round the yoke of the dress she wore for their visit to Summerside. The dress itself was printed silk with full sleeves, trimmed at collar, yoke, cuffs and hem with yellow silk. That evening, she changed into more casual clothes for a trotting meeting at Charlottetown, a pink, pale blue and white, striped mandarin, quilted jacket worn with a straight, pleated white skirt and pink court shoes.

Another favourite came out for the visit to Edmonton – the bright red suit with the white collar first seen in Port Pirie in Australia. Again, this dress is a sign of her ability to wear strong and contrasting colours, and clothes that 'can be seen'.

The invitation for a barbecue at Fort Edmonton read 'Dress semi-formal, Klondike era' and the Prince and Princess of Wales rose to the occasion. Prince Charles wore a frock coat, striped grey trousers and spats similar to those worn by his great-great grandfather, Edward VII, when he, as Prince of Wales, had visited the same area in 1878.

ABOVE: *the Chelsea Design Company created this silk dress with bold red spots that the Princess of Wales wore in both Australia and Canada. Over the dress she wore a red jacket edged in white silk braid with elbow-length sleeves. Matching red and white accessories completed the look.*

FACING PAGE: *For the last day in Newfoundland the Princess of Wales wore a classically styled, cobalt blue, cashmere coat. Contrasting with the blue were black buttons, collar, cuffs and pockets and a simple black sombrero hat which she has worn on several occasions with different outfits.*

Another new sailor suit for the Canadian tour but this time it was more formal in style. Made of lilac-grey silk, it had a drop waist with a narrow-pleated skirt. The distinctive sailor collar was in white silk and softly scalloped.

This stylish suit in raspberry pink from Jasper Conran was brought out of the wardrobe again for the Canadian tour. Its plain mandarin collar echoes the higher mandarin collar of the white silk shirt. The jacket is fastened at the side with transparent buttons.

The style of the clothes worn then also suited the present Princess of Wales beautifully. For the occasion, she had borrowed a long peach silk and cream dress with a lace underskirt and bustle. Ribbons, pink roses and pearls adorned the small, lace-trimmed hat and long, lace-up boots completed the picture. It was a very pretty dress and the close-fitted bodice and bustle accentuated her small waist. It had been borrowed from the BBC where it had been worn by Francesca Annis in her role as Lillie Langtry.

When her husband was conferred with an honorary Doctorate of Law from Alberta University the Princess of Wales, always mindful about clashing, wore the same blue and white, floral-printed dress from Donald Campbell's salon that she had worn in Brisbane. On this occasion, it was Prince Charles who wore one of his wife's favourite combinations of colour – bright red with white trimming.

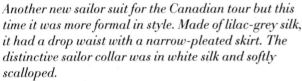

This grey and blue printed silk dress with striking yellow trimmings on the bodice, cuffs and at the hem was worn to Prince Edward Island. Yellow is another colour that suits the Princess of Wales, particularly for hats. The pretty, small bowler hat with its sweeping ostrich feather was in the same yellow as used in the dress.

The day of their departure from Canada, 1 July, was also the Princess's twenty-second birthday. For their tumultuous send-off from what was yet another highly successful tour, the Princess looked lovely in her silk, navy dress with magenta dots and mandarin collar. With it, she wore a magenta, bolero-style, quilted cashmere jacket with full sleeves and a straw hat.

Such a rich variety of clothes and colours were greatly admired throughout the two tours of the Prince and Princess of Wales. On their return to London, the great trunks were unpacked and, the clothes cleaned and put away by the Princess's lady's maid, Evelyn Dagley. Few were forgotten for long as the Princess, ever mindful of their cost, brought them out for her public engagements at home during the months that followed.

What then do we learn about the 'fashion' princess and what did she learn herself on her highly successful tours? First of all, in a variety of weathers and temperatures she had to have flexibility. She needed clothes which looked cool even in the heat of central Australia and coats to keep her warm and dry in the New Zealand rain. She learnt, too, that on television and in photographs, it is the simple, clean designs that work best, and what might seem a little

This favourite Jan Van Velden design was worn in both Australia and in Canada. The Princess of Wales has a marvellous ability for wearing strong, bright colours with striking fashion features such as this bold white collar with pointed edges. Note how the theme is repeated at the jacket hem.

exaggerated close to, on the screen looks marvellously eye-catching. She learned that 'theatrical' clothes work for her but that they have to be worn boldly. Edward VII would have admired her taste in clothes – strong and simple, even when she was not deliberately dressed like his favourite actress, Lillie Langtry.

The tours seemed to be the metamorphosis for the Princess. Her apprenticeship was over – as the fashionable princess the romantic little-girl look was no longer the right image. Here was the young mother, vigorous and in love with life and her clothes on the tours reflected this mood perfectly.

ABOVE: *The invitation for a barbecue at Fort Edmonton requested 'Dress of the Klondike era'. The Princess of Wales borrowed a peach silk and cream dress from the BBC and looked magnificent. The small hat was adorned with ribbons, pink roses and pearls and long, lace-up boots added a final touch.*

FACING PAGE: *For the journey home from Canada, the day of her 22nd birthday, the Princess of Wales wore a striking magenta and navy outfit. The plain magenta jacket was of quilted cashmere; the large, navy blue, straw hat was trimmed with a single feather falling rakishly down her back.*

OFF DUTY

'Off duty' to the Princess of Wales means 'off duty' and, as such, she can dress accordingly. That is not to say that she goes completely wild when out of the public eye, but she can at least wear what she likes and clothes in which she is most comfortable.

There is a fine line drawn between her dress on less formal official events and the smarter of her private occasions. She will wear a dress or a suit to a private function that will sometimes appear later at a public engagement, such as the pink, quilted suit she wore for the wedding of her friend Diana Chamberlayne-Macdonald to James Lindesay-Bethune which was then seen later on at the arrival of Queen Beatrix of the Netherlands on her State Visit to Britain. However, the bright pink, baggy sailor suit with a broad white collar which she wore for her former flatmate, Carolyn Pride's wedding has never been seen again. Not so the pretty, pink, flowered dress from Bellville Sassoon worn for Prince William's christening which reappeared during the tour of Australia. Rarely does the Princess of Wales wear her clothes the other way round – her 'working wardrobe' in her everyday life. The exceptions are the less formal clothes, such as the white blouse printed with heavy, black brush-strokes she wore in Adelaide which she sometimes wears with white cotton trousers to watch polo. It is the mark of how little the Princess of Wales has changed since her marriage in that her casual clothes are still identical to the style of her unmarried days. At Highgrove, her home in Gloucestershire, and on the Royal estates of Balmoral and Sandringham she still wears jeans and dungarees, bright, floral cotton shirts, T-shirts, still from Benetton, and colourful sweaters.

Inhabitants of her local town of Tetbury, or Ballater, the closest town to Balmoral, are used to seeing 'their' Princess driving herself to the shops, wearing her blue, straight-legged jeans, low pumps, probably her husband's 'V'-necked pullover and shirt (both ordered dozens from his shirt-maker, Turnbull and Asser, in Jermyn Street, London) and a blue Husky waistcoat. Besides her jeans, the Princess also wears culottes and dungarees to the same chic effect. However, the yellow pair that she occasionally used to wear to polo, with a flowered cotton blouse, have not been seen again although the Provençal quilted bag from Brother Sun is still much in use.

Those polo, and Princess, watchers well know her penchant for bright and exciting sweaters. One favourite sweater worn more than all the others before and after her marriage is her red, hand-knitted sweater covered with many white sheep and one individually placed black sheep on the right side. It came from a London shop, Warm and Wonderful, and was designed by Joanna Osborne and Sally Muir, the daughter of the television humorist Frank

The Princess of Wales is now becoming experienced at adapting her less formal clothes for many occasions. This white blouse with bold black brush-strokes has been dressed up with a smart hat and jewellery for a garden party in New Zealand but also looks informal for an afternoon watching Prince Charles play polo.

The off-duty Princess of Wales is mostly seen on the edge of the polo ground when she is watching Prince Charles. Her sense of colour and fashion is as keen on these occasions as when she is on-duty at her many and varied public engagements.

ABOVE: *Colourful hand-knits have always been a favourite of the Princess of Wales. This navy blue sweater was one of a pair presented to the Prince and Princess of Wales as wedding presents from Australia. The design has a large, grey koala bear climbing up the front and a map of Australia on the back.*

LEFT: *With her slim figure the Princess of Wales has always made the most simple, casual clothes look stylish. Jeans and dungarees particularly suit the Princess, as seen here before her marriage in a flowered, cotton blouse, yellow dungarees and espadrilles. Today her opportunities for wearing such clothes are limited.*

Muir. Penelope Keith and David Bowie have the same sweater in different colours. That sweater was the making of their shop. Joanna Osborne later admitted '. . . it really helped our business . . . in fact it is still selling, although the Princess wore it before she got married. We are trying hard to do other things but we can't get away from the sheep sweater.' Another particularly colourful sweater was one of a pair of wedding presents knitted and given by Kim Wran, the daughter of the then Premier of New South Wales, Australia. It was a particularly stylish number in navy blue with a grey koala bear climbing up the front and a map of Australia on the

back. In the spring of 1982, when she was over six months pregnant, she wore it with a frilled shirt and red corduroy trousers or just jeans. Another more recent favourite is a navy cardigan with a busy clouds and lightning design on the front and back and on the sleeves.

It has been said that the Prince of Wales likes to see his wife without stockings. When she dispensed with stockings at a Garden Party at Buckingham Palace it caused a certain unmerited comment. However, at polo one day, her slim, tanned legs were much admired beneath her smart 'city' grey, cuffed knee-length shorts, worn with a frilled blouse and

bright red sweater, invariably knotted about the neck.

For the smarter polo matches, like those on Sundays at Smith's Lawn and Cowdray Park, the Princess wears what she has lunched in, and that generally comes under the heading of informally smart. One such dress was a white shirtwaister with red, blue and green polka-dots with a white belt, worn in July 1983.

On the Prince and Princess of Wales's brief moments of relaxation during the tour of Australia, the Princess did watch Prince Charles play polo at Warwick Farm. Under her umbrella and navy blue blazer, she wore another of her sailor dresses from

The Chelsea Design Company. Blue and white striped, it had a long-line bodice on a dropped waist with long ties at the front from the large collar.

Not long after Christmas 1981, the Princess switched to maternity dresses. Ever practical, she had many made up at a time, all of similar style but of different colours. They were all loose fitting and flowing – silk for the grander occasions, cotton for everyday wear. Some had plain collars and others, such as the cornflower blue dress she wore at Aintree for the Grand National, had pie-crust collars. The majority, however, had white shawl collars tied in an exaggerated bow at the front. They were in pinks

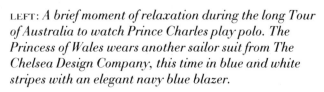

LEFT: *A brief moment of relaxation during the long Tour of Australia to watch Prince Charles play polo. The Princess of Wales wears another sailor suit from The Chelsea Design Company, this time in blue and white stripes with an elegant navy blue blazer.*

BELOW LEFT: *Many of the Princess of Wales's off-duty maternity dresses continued the sailor-suit theme with large, white shawl collars tied in an exaggerated bow at the front. This dress from The Chelsea Design Company was made in a blue and white, check, lightweight silk.*

BELOW RIGHT: *Identical in style to the blue and white check dress, this green and white polka-dot dress became the most famous of all her maternity dresses as it was the one she wore to leave the hospital, so soon after the birth of Prince William.*

FACING PAGE: *Seen for the first time in July 1983, this dress was worn for a smarter polo match after lunch on Sunday. Styled with one of the Princess's favourite themes, a plain white collar and cuffs, the white shirt-waisted dress had bright red, blue and green polka-dots and was tied with a soft, white leather belt at the waist.*

When north of the border, the Princess of Wales often dresses in a Scottish style. For this Highland Gathering at Braemar she is wearing a dark green, plaid dress from Caroline Charles with striking white moiré silk collar and cuffs. Her hat is a Glengarry, the traditional head-dress of Scottish regiments.

and light blues, they were plain, they were checked and undoubtedly the most famous one was the green and white, polka-dot dress with the white collar which she wore when she carried out Prince William from hospital, only hours after he was born.

A departure from her usual silks, cottons and wool mixtures for her suits was one in emerald-green suede trimmed with punched, gold leather which she wore to attend a concert at Tetbury Church. It was typical of the designer, Jean Muir, a doyenne of the British fashion scene for decades.

An obvious area where the Princess's 'private' wardrobe can be examined in detail is in the official photographs. Taken in her own home surroundings and consequently in a more relaxed atmosphere, these photographs are indicative of her own personal, as opposed to public, style – from the earliest, the well-known Inca sweater, corduroy knickerbockers

tucked into pink socks and green Hunter boots of her engagement days seen at Balmoral, to the latest informal session with Prince William and his father at their apartments in Kensington Palace. For that session, the Princess changed twice. For the photographs with Prince William, she wore a grey and white, drop-waisted pinafore dress in grey and white crêpe-de-Chine over a printed white silk shirt. For the photographs with Prince Charles, she chose a dark apricot crêpe-de-Chine shirtwaisted dress with a white frilled collar, a silk bow and matching white collar and cuffs (see page 57). For an earlier photo session with Prince William, she wore a red, short-sleeved, sailor-style dress trimmed in white and worn over a silk, frilly blouse.

Another traditional opportunity to see the Royal Family is on their way to and from Balmoral and at the Highland Gathering at Braemar. There, the Princess of Wales is generally seen in one of her favourites, either the Caroline Charles red or the green plaid dress worn either with a tam o' shanter or a Glengarry. For the 1983 Highland Gathering she switched to her green velvet suit with the pin-tucked sleeves as she had worn her plaid dress to visit a sweet factory in Dundee earlier in the month.

Official photographs are taken of the Royal Family in the comfortable surroundings of their home atmosphere. This session taken in the private apartments of Kensington Palace shows a relaxed Princess of Wales wearing a grey and white, drop-waisted pinafore dress with a printed white silk blouse underneath.

A relaxed Lady Diana Spencer at Balmoral with Prince Charles. These casual, comfortable clothes – the well-known, pink Inca sweater, corduroy knickerbockers tucked into long pink socks and green Hunter boots – are indicative of her own personal style as opposed to her public style, a distinction which she still makes today.

EVENING WEAR

Strict protocol dictates that members of the Royal Family are always the last to arrive at any function, especially an evening one. Thus they are assured, whether they like it or not, that all eyes, including the photographers' lenses, are upon them at their entrance. If the member of the Royal Family is the Princess of Wales, that interest is heightened. Although she invariably looks her best for her daytime functions, she is undeniably even more elegant for those evening engagements.

As with her day clothes, the Princess is not afraid to experiment, within bounds, with style and colour, regardless of any real or supposed 'Buckingham Palace strictures'. However, evening dresses are very much more expensive and therefore not open to too much experimenting, even with a fabulous dress allowance. Because of their expense and prettiness, and the increasing number of evening engagements, she is often seen in the same evening dresses, sometimes in rapid succession.

By the time of her marriage, the Princess of Wales knew her way round the top fashion houses of London. The editors of *Vogue* put her in touch with others, the young up-and-coming designers or the more established ones who could provide her with what she wanted. Those whom she had patronised before have an exact record of her size and can gauge her taste. New designers, of course, have to measure her up themselves and discuss their ideas with her. She will either visit their salon in person to see their range or, now more often, they will go to see her at Kensington Palace. Sometimes, Anna Harvey from *Vogue* will be there too, to co-ordinate their ideas. The designer will make many sketches before exactly the right style and shape emerges; swatches of material will be examined minutely until the right colour and texture is chosen to fit the design. Depending on how soon the dress is needed, it will be ready for the first fitting in around ten days – longer if complicated, sooner if needed in a hurry. The dress will be tacked together but well enough to see the fit and how the style is shaping. When the adjustments are made with pins, the dress will be sent back to the workrooms to be finished off. Sometimes there is more than one fitting if the dress is not right, but the Princess's designers generally succeed the first time.

On occasions, as in the early days at the Emanuels, the Princess will choose a 'shell' – that is a dress that has been made up loosely and which can be fitted and made up, sometimes in a matter of hours. She may also see a dress that she likes and have it made up in a different colour. It is impracticable for her to buy an evening dress 'off the peg', however much she likes it, as she could never guarantee that there would not be that awful moment when two identical

dresses meet. Because of the material and style, copies of her evening dresses are expensive and it would be unlikely that anyone, knowing that they are to meet or be at the same reception as the Princess, would be tactless enough to wear their copy.

Since her marriage, the Princess of Wales has tried many different styles and designers for her evening clothes, and with minor variations on a central theme, she has developed a more distinct style for evening dresses than for her daytime clothes. She is altogether more confident in the wearing of her evening dresses, sometimes even bold in her choice, such as the two 'off the shoulder' dresses.

The Princess keeps all her dresses: some are brought out years after their first wearing or kept for the more formal dinners at home or with other members of the Royal Family. One such dress that she has had from before her marriage is the gold-spangled, red chiffon dress with the ruched bodice that she first wore for the première of the James Bond film *For Your Eyes Only* at the Odeon, Leicester Square, in aid of the National Society for

At Covent Garden where she met Rudolf Nureyev the Princess of Wales wore one of the evening dresses she had had made during her engagement. Designed by Bellville Sassoon it was made of gold-spangled red chiffon. It was beautifully complemented by a diamond and gold necklace and pendant with Prince of Wales feathers.

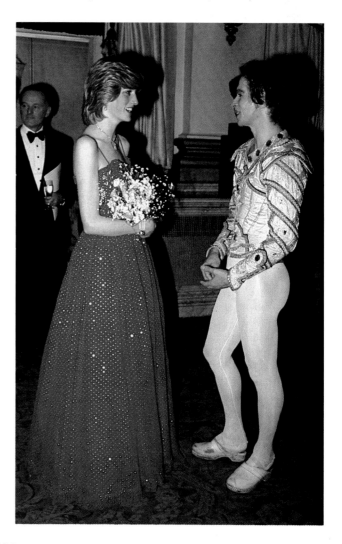

FACING PAGE: *One of the first evening dresses seen after her marriage was this Donald Campbell, deep blue, silk chiffon, short evening dress with a leaf motif shot with gold thread. The top half of the bodice was softly ruched and the neck shirred with a pie-crust collar. The silk cummerbund had two large bows at the front.*

the Prevention of Cruelty to Children and the Royal Association for Disability and Rehabilitation. Then she wore a borrowed ruby and diamond choker and bracelet, but, nearly two years later when she wore the same dress for a visit to the Royal Opera House, Covent Garden, she wore the necklace with the Prince of Wales feathers and her five-strand pearl bracelet with sapphire clasp. Another evening dress worn before and after her wedding was the Nettie Vogues' dark emerald-green, silk taffeta dress she wore for her engagement photograph. The dress, with its square neck, puffed sleeves and balloon skirt, was next seen during the Tour of Wales in October 1981 at a gala evening in Swansea. Likewise, the pale blue, silk chiffon evening dress that she, as Lady Diana Spencer, had worn for the banquet given by King Khaled of Saudia Arabia at Claridges, came out again for the visit to the opening of the new theatre in Cardiff for a performance by the Welsh National Opera of which she is Patron (see page 116). Also in Cardiff on the last day of her first Tour of Wales, she wore a deep-blue, silk chiffon dress with a leaf motif shot with gold thread. The sleeves were full, the shoulders ruched and the neck shirred with a pie-crust collar. The Donald Campbell dress was drawn into the waist by a silk cummerbund with two bows. With it, she wore a black velvet cape lined with white satin from Gina Fratini.

Not strictly an evening dress, but nonetheless long, is the special dress which the Princess of Wales wears to the State Opening of Parliament. She wore it first on 4 November 1981, her first State occasion as Princess of Wales and has subsequently worn it every year since. The deep V-necked dress is of silk organza with an overlay of stylised flowers in silver and is generally worn with long, white gloves, a pearl choker and the Queen Mary tiara. The full sleeves to the elbow also have a similar silver overlay.

Possibly the most photographed item of all the Princess's large wardrobe is the magnificent Bellville Sassoon, hand-painted, silk chiffon evening dress of the palest pinks and blues which she wore to the

FACING PAGE: *By far the most famous of all the Princess of Wales's evening dresses is this magnificent hand-painted, silk chiffon dress in soft blues and pinks on a white background from Bellville Sassoon. Tiny silver beads were sewn onto the material to give a shimmering effect. A satin sash and bows completed the romantic look.*

BELOW: *In her position as third lady in the land after the Queen and Queen Mother, the Princess of Wales has a part to play on all state occasions. Her first appearance in such a role was at the State Opening of Parliament in November 1981. The white silk organza dress is worn with long white gloves and her most grand tiara.*

ABOVE LEFT AND RIGHT: *Gina Fratini has designed many of the Princess of Wales's most successful evening dresses, including the heavy velvet green dress with a lace puritan collar and attached lace petticoat. The Princess of Wales has worn this dress on several occasions, including to this charity concert in Manchester.*

opening of The Splendours of the Gonzaga exhibition at the Victoria and Albert. It was an entrancing dress that suited her well with its off-the-shoulder neckline with satin bows and a very full skirt. On that occasion, she wore her six-strand pearl choker, but when she wore the dress again for the première of the film *Gandhi*, a year later, she wore her necklace with the Prince of Wales feathers.

Almost by contrast to the ethereal quality of this dress was the heavy velvet green dress she wore to the twenty-fifth London Film Festival. Designed by Gina Fratini, it had a delicate lace puritan collar and attached lace petticoat. The long sleeves were full and the waist sashed. Also in velvet was the rich, ink-blue dress by Bellville Sassoon that she wore to dine at 11 Downing Street in early February 1982. It was a romantic Stuart-style dress with its Empire lines and long lace collars and matching cuffs. It was the first time that she had worn the magnificent sapphire brooch, a present from the Saudi Royal Family. Not to overdo her jewellery, she wore just the sapphire pendant necklace with the same dress in December for a charity concert at the Festival Hall.

During the spring of 1982, the more strenuous of the evening engagements were kept to a minimum for the Princess was half-way through her pregnancy. For a relatively relaxed evening engagement at the Royal Albert Hall for a performance of Berlioz's *Grande Messe des Morts,* sung by the Bach Choir, Bellville Sassoon had created a dress in red chiffon flecked with gold, with the neck and tight cuffs edged in gold braid. Another red evening dress and another musical evening was when the Prince and Princess of Wales visited the Barbican Centre. On that occasion, she wore a striking, heavy silk taffeta, ruby evening dress by Bellville Sassoon. The square neckline was edged in lace as were the cuffs.

It was a study in white when the Princess met Elizabeth Taylor, the star of *The Little Foxes* at the Victoria Palace Theatre. Bellville Sassoon had designed the white georgette evening dress worn with her white mink jacket.

After the birth of Prince William and the subsequent traditional summer and autumn holiday of the Royal Family at Balmoral, the Princess made a dramatic return to public life with a remarkable evening dress for a charity fashion show at the Guildhall, in the City of London. The novel electric-blue, one-shouldered silk dress with its frilled top and bow at the side and dropped waist was designed by Bruce Oldfield: a talented English designer whose work is known on both sides of the Atlantic.

FACING PAGE: *Bellville Sassoon designed this silk taffeta, ruby evening dress for the Princess of Wales to wear during her pregnancy. The square neckline with its froth of lace was cleverly designed to attract attention.*

Soon after the arrival of Queen Beatrix of The Netherlands for her State Visit, the Princess of Wales, among others of the Royal Family, was presented with the Order of the House of Orange. The dress that she had singled out to wear for the banquet at Hampton Court that night would have clashed horribly with the bright orange and white silk sash and a hasty substitute was found. This was of white chiffon lined with white satin with full sleeves gathered at the elbow.

A slight departure from colour, was the Roland Klein dress that she wore for the première of the film *E.T.* The strapless dress had a tightly fitting damson velvet bodice with a full taffeta plaid skirt, sashed at the waist with the same material.

By the time of the Royal Tours of Australia and New Zealand in the spring of 1983 and then of Canada in the summer, the Princess had very definite ideas about what she wanted from her evening dresses. Months of planning and fittings were rewarded with a stunning collection of dresses, nine of which were worn over the two tours. The honour of the first evening dress went to Murray

BELOW: *Bruce Oldfield designed the first one-shouldered dress worn by the Princess of Wales. It was a complete departure from her normal classic style and was exotic in both its effect and colour with its electric blue print and dropped waist. Of all her designers Bruce Oldfield has profited the most from the Princess's patronage.*

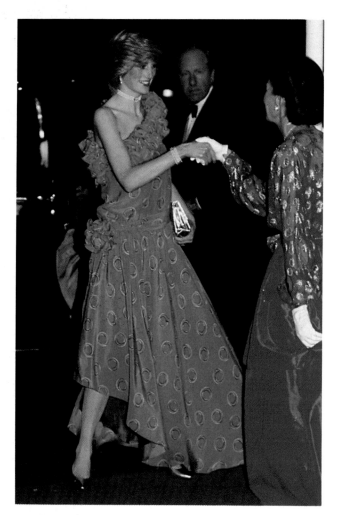

ABOVE: *In a new colour for the Princess of Wales was this damson, strapless dress designed by Roland Klein. This designer has a wonderful ability of mixing colourways and materials, such as here with his use of both velvet and silk – the bodice is made of velvet and the full skirt is made of a silk taffeta plaid.*

Arbeid, one of the foremost designers in London, who specialises in grand evening dresses. For dinner at Government House in Canberra she wore a beautiful, yellow-gold, silk taffeta dress with leg-of-mutton sleeves and a dropped waist. She had worn the dress before at a charity evening at Sadler's Wells Theatre in London and later, she wore it on the Royal Tour of Canada, in St John, New Brunswick. Although she wore the Family Order on both occasions, she changed her jewellery, the Spencer tiara and the Saudi Arabian sapphires for Australia, the Queen Mary tiara and her heart choker for the Canadians.

For Sydney, it was a Bruce Oldfield dress of pale blue, ruffled silk georgette striped with silver thread. The sleeves were short and the dress was worn with a tight, silver, leather cummerbund belt. As the

FACING PAGE: *The honour of designing the first evening dress for the Tour of Australia went to Murray Arbeid who is famed for his extravagant evening wear. This yellow-gold, silk taffeta dress had a V-necked, pin-tucked bodice with leg-of-mutton sleeves and a fashionable dropped waist.*

For the state banquet in New Brunswick on the Tour of Canada the Princess of Wales wore a Bruce Oldfield dress of blue and silver silk georgette cinched at the waist with a wide, silver, leather cummerbund. Soft ruffles at the shoulders and down the sides of the dress added to the shimmering effect.

Another dress that was worn in both Australia and Canada was this one of shocking pink organza that showed off the Princess of Wales's marvellous figure to perfection. The soft tucks on the bodice were repeated lower down the skirt and narrow ribbon straps at the shoulders were covered with soft bows.

Created by The Chelsea Design Company, this dress was typical of the Princess of Wales's more romantic style. Worn to a variety concert in Melbourne, it was made of an enchanting rose-pink silk with a gold circle motif. The theme of gold was repeated in the large bow at the waist and in the frilled sleeves and neckline.

occasion was a grand ball, as opposed to a State occasion, she did not wear a tiara. Nonetheless, the full diamond necklace and drop, single-pearl earrings enhanced the dress. In Canada she wore the same dress with the Spencer tiara and the miniature of the Queen at a state banquet in St John, New Brunswick. Red was much in evidence in the Princess's clothes for their visit to Hobart. For the Tasmanian State Reception, she chose another evening dress by Bruce Oldfield. Made of scarlet, silver-spotted chiffon it had a deep-frilled neckline and was flounced at the hem (see page 125).

Possibly the finest of all her evening dresses from both tours is the one she wore for the Queensland State reception. It was one of two designed by Victor Edelstein, whom the Princess had met through her *Vogue* contacts and whose work she had admired. Although she took two dresses designed by him on the tour, the one seen was of shocking pink organza with a tight-pleated bodice, ribbon straps with bows at the shoulder. Later in the year, September, she wore the same dress to the Barry Manilow concert at the Royal Festival Hall.

The Chelsea Design Company, who had already produced so many of her daytime clothes, designed the rose pink and gold-circle motif evening dress she wore for a variety concert at Melbourne towards the end of her tour. This pretty dress was sashed at the peplum waist and had a low-frilled neckline and balloon sleeves gathered at the elbow. The white, sequined, one-shouldered dress that the Princess of Wales wore for the end of the tour of Australia at a charity farewell ball certainly caused a stir. It was a tightly fitting dress and the stark lines were a complete departure from her usual flounces and frills. It was designed by Hachi, a Japanese designer who had been working for some years in England. Renowned for his 'brilliantly cut, often sensationally beaded, evening dresses', the Princess certainly knew that he could provide what she was looking for; Hachi commented, 'I am thrilled with this one.' Melbourne certainly had not seen the like. Back in London, she wore the same evening dress for the première of the James Bond film, *Octopussy*.

Donald Campbell designed the off-the-shoulder periwinkle taffeta evening dress with its tightly fitted bodice and full skirt which the Princess wore to attend the ballet in Auckland. It was a colour that suited her well. Another new dress for New Zealand, later to be seen in Halifax, Nova Scotia, on the Canadian tour, came from Gina Fratini in cream silk with a pin-tucked bodice and a sashed waist. The elbow-length sleeves were full and, like the pretty neckline, were trimmed with lace.

Although the Canadians had seen most of her evening dresses before from the Tour of Australia and New Zealand, they looked stunning and somewhat different when worn with different pieces of jewellery. However, the Canadians did have one original evening dress for their visit, worn at a farewell banquet at Government House, Edmonton. The dress was bright red in colour by Jan Van

Velden, with a transparent lace organza top over a silk taffeta bodice and matching full skirt.

With these evening dresses from the two tours, and the ones that she had made and never wore, the Princess of Wales is well set up for some time to come. She does, of course, have other evening dresses that are not generally seen in public, such as a white silk dress she wears with a Royal Stuart sash for the Ghillies' Ball at Balmoral every September.

BELOW: *Although Jan Van Velden designed many day clothes for the Princess of Wales to wear on her long overseas tours in 1983, he only designed one evening dress – this one in bright red silk taffeta. The transparent lace organza top with sequins covered the taffeta bodice which had narrow straps. The full skirt was plain.*

ABOVE: *For the last evening of the Australia Tour the Princess of Wales chose a new style that was a complete departure from her more usual romantic look. Designed by Hachi, a Japanese designer working in England, it was a slim-fitting, one-shouldered dress made of white beaded material which emphasised her wonderful figure.*

FACING PAGE: *Designed by Gina Fratini for formal evenings, this dress was worn by the Princess of Wales both in New Zealand and Canada, with a tiara and dazzling jewellery on both occasions. The cream silk, organza dress was trimmed with narrow lace and satin ribbons on the pin-tucked bodice and sleeves.*

JEWELLERY

Although the Princess of Wales does not, of course, need fantastic jewellery to sparkle and be noticed, the pieces belonging to her, and those at her disposal, are magnificent and undeniably add yet another dimension to her overall loveliness. Like all girls of her position and background, she had access to more jewellery than she actually owned in her own right – family jewellery of the aristocracy is usually entailed with the estate, that is, passed down through the eldest son and heir. Before her marriage, her own pieces were modest. Although girls at West Heath were not allowed to wear anything other than studs or sleepers in their pierced ears, the rule was generally relaxed and Lady Diana was no exception. There, she wore a simple three-strand, Russian wedding ring, a silver bracelet and a gold letter 'D' on a chain that her friends had clubbed together to buy her as a birthday present. She still wears these simpler pieces today, including a gold and lapis enamelled flower brooch. While at West Heath, she went into nearby Sevenoaks to have her ears pierced, in a shop called Adam and Eve. Little was added to

FACING PAGE: For her many formal evening occasions, when she must look at her most glamorous, the Princess of Wales can draw upon one of the finest collections of jewellery in the world, the Royal collection, as well as upon her own family pieces known as the 'Spencer pool', such as the Spencer diamond tiara she is wearing here.

BELOW: This gold letter 'D' on a chain was given to Lady Diana Spencer when she was still at school by a group of friends. Before her engagement she would often wear it with simple, gold, hooped earrings. Nowadays when the Princess of Wales wears it on informal occasions she wears it with a longer gold chain.

this basic collection before her engagement, anything she needed simply being borrowed from family or friends.

The Royal Wedding was very much a traditional and family affair. Like her sisters, Lady Jane and Lady Sarah before her, Lady Diana wore the Spencer family tiara for her own wedding. The early nineteenth-century 'Spencer tiara' is a beautiful piece, diamonds mounted on a gold and silver base in a foliate design. The wearing of tiaras dates from the neo-classical period (late eighteenth and early nineteenth-century), being modelled on the classical diadem, a head-piece with a front but no back. Before then, the ladies at Court wore either mounted gem stones in their hair, circlets or small coronets. Tiaras became a popular adornment throughout the nineteenth and early twentieth centuries. Like today, they were worn at Court and every grand occasion but then, obviously, more frequently than today.

The Spencer tiara has been worn many times since the Royal Wedding by the Princess of Wales, on occasions such as the State Opening of Parliament or the Royal Tours of Australia and Canada (at Hobart, Brisbane and New Brunswick). The other tiara that the Princess of Wales wears was given to her by the Queen as a wedding present. It was given to the Queen by her grandmother, Queen Mary, as a wedding present on her marriage in 1947 – the Queen always referred to it as 'Granny's tiara'. Of the two, this is the one seen most often on the grandest of occasions, such as the formal banquet at Hampton Court for the State Visit of Queen Beatrix of The Netherlands or throughout the recent tours of the Commonwealth.

The Royal 'jewel pool' (as opposed to the Crown Jewels which belong to the state not the monarch) is vast and magnificent. Much of the Queen's jewellery has either been inherited or given to her over the years as Sovereign and some of these important pieces are borrowed for specific occasions by her daughter-in-law.

Lady Diana's drop diamond earrings worn for her wedding came from 'the Fermoy (her mother's family) pool', as opposed to the 'Spencer family pool'. Since then, she has acquired many sets of earrings of her own, mostly as gifts. It is a wide range, too, from those of that fabulous set of sapphires, a gift from the Saudi Arabian Royal Family, down to a simple pair of gold, hooped earrings.

The Princess likes wearing jewellery. One fashion writer observed, ' . . . she is wearing the most marvellous sapphires and diamond earrings with her little woollies and sweaters. It is a sort of inverse joke that she carries off the real thing as though it were paste.' The particular earrings the writer referred to were a pair of pear-shaped diamond drops with interchangeable centres of sapphires and rubies.

The plain gold, hooped earrings, some set with diamonds, are usually just worn by her at home, as

The Princess of Wales now has a vast array of earrings to choose from: she often wears diamond ones during the day as well as in the evening. For the Snowdon photograph taken to mark her 21st birthday, she wore some lovely pear-shaped, diamond drops which have interchangeable centres of either sapphires or rubies.

This is the same pair of earrings as on the left but this time the ruby centres have been put in to match the bright red, silk suit worn by the Princess of Wales. The three-stranded pearl choker has a pearl and turquoise clasp which can be turned to the back of the neck whenever turquoise does not match the colour of her outfit.

are the pair of rock crystal and gold, drop earrings worn for the official photographs of the Prince and Princess of Wales with Prince William taken in Kensington Palace in February 1982.

Whatever the pundits say of the Princess as a leader of fashion with her clothes, no one can deny the effect that she has had on jewellery, especially pearl chokers. Christina Miste-Ireland, a spokeswoman for the jewellery trade, said, 'After the first pearl choker was seen on the Princess of Wales, there was a fantastic demand for not only copies to sell for a few pounds but a rush for the real thing as well. Granny's pearls took on a new lease of life as they were restrung into chokers.' Despite these imitations, the Princess has not only remained faithful to her favourite chokers, but now has others of varying sizes. Not strictly a choker, she has always had a single string of pearls. She has now inherited many others, one with a diamond and sapphire clasp. Like all her pearl necklaces, she can wear them with the clasp showing or not, depending on what she is wearing. For example, the turquoise and gold clasp on her three-strand pearl choker has been worn on

many occasions, sometimes to the front, sometimes to the back such as during her first Tour of Wales, where the turquoise would have clashed with the deep burgundy colour of her suit. The gold and pavé diamonds of her pretty, four-strand pearl choker, first seen for the State banquet at Hampton Court, is an important piece and definitely not to be worn to the back. Another piece, once borrowed from the 'Spencer pool', is the five-strand pearl choker with a large pearl and diamond clasp with a further drop pearl from that. It was instantly noticed that it was worn by the Princess's sister, Lady Sarah, for the wedding and photographs and appeared just a few hours later on the Princess of Wales's neck as she left Buckingham Palace on the start of her honeymoon. One strand up, at six strands, is a fine choker with a

FACING PAGE: *Another tiara often worn by the Princess of Wales was given to her by the Queen as a wedding present. It is known as 'Granny's tiara' as it once belonged to Queen Mary. The necklace of cultured pearls set in diamonds with a heart-shaped locket was a present from Prince Charles on the birth of Prince William.*

114

Necklaces

RIGHT: The Princess of Wales at her most glittering. Wearing a romantic-styled sequined evening dress designed by the Emanuels, the shimmering effect of the sequins is enhanced by the lustre of the magnificent, single-strand pearl necklace, the large, pear-shaped diamond earrings and the Spencer tiara. BELOW: An enchanting necklace of small cultured pearls set in diamonds with a heart-shaped locket was a romantic present from Prince Charles on the birth of Prince William. FACING PAGE: The Princess of Wales has access to the unrivalled collection of Royal jewels belonging to the Queen and often wears pieces from it when she wishes to really sparkle. One such piece is this dazzling diamond necklace known within the Royal Family as 'Granny's chips' – the stones were cut from the famous Cullinan diamond which the Queen inherited from her grandmother, Queen Mary.

heavy pearl and diamond clasp that she enjoys wearing – it goes particularly well with the Queen Mary tiara and was first worn by her at the State Opening of Parliament on 4 November 1981.

Obviously not worn as often as the daytime jewellery, but even more spectacular, are the Princess's diamond, sapphire and emerald necklaces. This exceptional collection has come either from wedding presents or from 'the Royal pool' – the Queen and Queen Elizabeth the Queen Mother. The last Prince of Wales, Edward VIII, gave many pieces from the Royal collection to his wife, the present Duchess of Windsor. However, it is thought that the Prince of Wales will eventually inherit them and so add them to the Princess's collection.

Before the wedding, the Spencer family had the embarrassment of not owning a diamond necklace suitable for an engagement photograph and, in royal, time-honoured fashion, borrowed a spectacular diamond necklace and drop earrings from one of the royal jewellers, Collingwood of Conduit Street, London. After the photographic session, the necklace and earrings were sold to an Arab who then sold them to a West German jeweller. He unceremoniously offered them 'as worn by the Lady Diana Spencer' with a copy of the engagement photograph to prove it. One of the wedding presents from her father, the Earl Spencer, was a jewel case (empty) – a prophetic present considering what she has been given to fill it and how often she has to use it on her travels. One wedding present that does not fit into her father's case is the fabulous wedding present from the Saudi Arabian Royal Family that has its own box of green malachite embossed in gold with the emblem of the Saudi Royal Family, a gold palm tree with crossed swords. Apart from the sapphire earrings already mentioned, there is a necklace, gold with diamonds, with a Burmese sapphire pendant also set in gold with diamonds; a matching ring, bracelet and watch complete the 'set'. It has to be a very grand affair to wear the whole 'set', and normally the Princess picks only one or two pieces to wear at a time. Also, from the Near East came a 'gold choker set with multicoloured gems and an antique Indian piece from the turn of the century' from the Crown Prince and Princess of Jordan.

Another treasured wedding present was from the National Association of Goldsmiths. Given a free choice, she chose a pavé-set diamond, white gold necklet with a pendant of diamond and sapphire flowers around Prince of Wales feathers. The designer, Lexi Dick, suggested a unicorn, but the Princess was adamant on her husband's crest.

The Royal Family undeniably appreciate and enjoy their fabulous collection of jewellery, but they are also modern in their thinking that it is the stones that count, not the settings if they are old-fashioned or impractical. One such example of stones being reused is the famous Cullinan diamond inherited from Queen Mary. The Queen had it recut into nine important diamonds and many other smaller stones, known within the Royal Family as 'granny's chips'.

These were set into a brilliant necklace that has also been worn by the Princess, as on her visit to the Barbican Centre in March 1982.

Also eminently suitable to the Princess's style and colour of evening dresses is the cabochon emerald and faceted diamond collier. This has proved a fine alternative to her diamond and sapphire pieces. Although not seen in public that often, she did wear it for the gala in Swansea, where she wore the emerald-green dress of her engagement photograph (see page 25).

Occasionally, the Princess wears a bracelet, generally to tie in with something else that she is wearing – the Saudi sapphires, a pearl choker or a diamond necklace. She has three stranded pearl bracelets, one with five strings, and a large diamond and pearl clasp is a favourite of hers for the evening. At home, and on less formal occasions, she wears a heavy, gold chain bracelet with a citrine charm on

FACING PAGE: *The Princess of Wales wearing the Spencer tiara with the magnificent sapphires presented to her as a wedding present from the Saudi Arabian Royal Family. The Princess rarely wears all the sapphires together; here she is wearing the earrings, necklace and bracelet.*

BELOW: *Pearls are the Sloane Ranger's favourite jewels and always look effective against a slightly tanned skin such as here during the Tour of Canada. The Princess of Wales has many different pearl necklaces, most of them inherited since her marriage. She often wears this single strand of beautiful pearls during the day time.*

her right wrist. However, she usually removes it if there is much handshaking ahead or if she is wearing a dress or blouse with a frilled wrist.

She has always worn her watch on her left wrist. Until her engagement, she wore a large and inexpensive man's watch with a leather strap. Knowing how much she liked that watch, Prince Charles gave her a rather more feminine replica in eighteen-carat gold, which she now wears practically all the time. For the evening, she alternates between two of her wedding presents, a watch set in a diamond and sapphire bracelet from the Crown Prince of Saudi Arabia and another from Sheikha Fatima of the United Arab Emirates.

Brooches are not normally worn by the Princess, apart from a few favourites or whenever they are necessary – one brooch, a large sapphire set with diamonds, was hurriedly fixed to the Order of Orange at the banquet at Hampton Court to stop the silk ribbon across her front from slipping. Another brooch that she occasionally wears, a cabochon sapphire set with diamonds, is occasionally seen in public, as on her visit to the Charlie Chaplin Adventure Playground in south London. Another, yet to be seen in public, is a pearl brooch, a present from the islanders of Fiji.

Shaking hundreds of hands a day is not conducive to the wearing of rings and, by lesson and experience, the Princess of Wales has kept her rings, in public, down to her wedding ring and her engagement ring. There was just enough gold left from the nugget found in Wales in the 1920s to make her wedding ring – the rest of the nugget had been used for the Queen Mother's in 1923, the Queen's in 1947, Princess Margaret's in 1960 and Princess Anne's in 1973. The engagement ring, a cabochon sapphire set with fourteen diamonds on a white gold ring, had been chosen by Lady Diana from several brought on approval from one of the Crown Jewellers, Garrard & Co. of Regent Street. After the engagement announcement copies were available in a matter of days from the 'real thing' down to paste costing a few pounds.

A charming tradition of the Royal Family is the granting of Family Orders, the most personal of all royal honours bestowed only on the immediate family of the Sovereign. The Royal Family Orders are known to date back to 1820 and George IV, and with the exception of King Edward VIII have been renewed each reign. The Elizabeth II Family Order is a miniature of the Queen within a border of brilliants

FACING PAGE: *The most sumptuous of the Princess of Wales's chokers is a six-strand one which she wears on grander occasions. Belonging to the Royal collection, it has a heavy diamond and pearl clasp. With it she is wearing some magnificent diamond, pear-shaped earrings.*

Pearls always look magnificent with black and white and, in order not to detract from the overall effect, the Princess of Wales has turned the turquoise clasp of this three-stranded choker to the back. She is also wearing a favourite pair of diamond and gold studs set with a large, single pearl.

BELOW: *Even before her marriage, the Princess of Wales's preference for pearl chokers was similar to that of her predecessor, Queen Alexandra whose famous pearl and velvet chokers became her trademark. Then, as now, there arose a fantastic demand for imitations as well as for the real thing.*

Earrings

Since her wedding the Princess of Wales has acquired many sets of earrings of her own, mostly as gifts. A favourite combination is sapphires and diamonds. RIGHT: This pair of earrings has not been seen often in public. The small diamond flowers have narrow sapphire drops hanging from them and complement the rich blue velvet suit and matching hat with deep blue eye veil. BELOW: A formal study of the Princess of Wales taken by Lord Snowdon shortly before her marriage. The diamond stars have a large, single sapphire in the centre. FACING PAGE: These diamond and gold hooped earrings are another favourite pair belonging to the Princess of Wales who often wears them with a simple pearl necklace.

ABOVE AND LEFT: *Sapphires complement the colour of the Princess of Wales's eyes and she loves wearing them in all shapes and forms. A useful feature of these sapphire and diamond earrings is that they can be worn either as a single earclip or as a double pendant.*

FACING PAGE: *With the Spencer tiara the Princess of Wales is wearing a diamond, white gold necklet with a pendant of flowers around Prince of Wales feathers and the Family Order bestowed on her by the Queen.*

and baguette diamonds. It is surmounted by a diamond-set Tudor Crown and three stone diamond loops, resting on a velvet cushion of red enamel. The riband is always of watered silk in a bow two inches wide in chartreuse yellow. The Orders are always worn on the left shoulder.

The Queen's badges are all made by Garrards, one of the Crown Jewellers and the pictures are painted on ivory. The Queen has bestowed her own Family Orders on the Queen Mother, Princess Anne, Princess Margaret, various of the female Royal cousins and now the Princess of Wales.

Beauty care

BELOW: Before her marriage the Princess of Wales had a simple hairstyle that emphasised the roundness of her face and she wore little or no make-up except for official photographs such as this one. RIGHT AND FACING PAGE: After her marriage she grew her hair slightly longer which showed off to great effect her new slimness. There has been no change to her hairstyle for the past two years except that it is a touch longer. There are no plans to change the style for the moment. At the start of a session, her hairdresser, Kevin Shanley always asks what she will be wearing on her head; with tiaras and smaller hats he does her hair tighter to accentuate the waviness. For larger hats or no hats at all Kevin has a free rein.

The new portrait of the Princess of Wales which was unveiled by the Princess at the end of January 1984. It was commissioned by The Worshipful Company of Grocers to hang in Grocers Hall. Painted by June Mendoza, the portrait depicts an up-to-date image of the Princess, looking elegant and self-confident. The Princess is wearing the bright red silk taffeta evening dress made for her by Jan Van Velden (see page 111) but a certain artist's licence has been used to tone down the colour and to soften the neckline in order to enhance the Princess's features and to give a greater effect against the dark red walls of the Livery Hall.